Electricity Distribution Networks
in the Decentralisation Era

Rahmatallah Poudineh · Christine Brandstätt ·
Farhad Billimoria

Electricity Distribution Networks in the Decentralisation Era

Rethinking Economics and Regulation

palgrave
macmillan

Rahmatallah Poudineh
Oxford Institute for Energy Studies
Oxford, UK

Farhad Billimoria
Oxford Institute for Energy Studies
Oxford, UK

Energy & Power Group
Department of Engineering Science
University of Oxford
Oxford, UK

Christine Brandstätt
Oxford Institute for Energy Studies
Oxford, UK

Copenhagen Business School
Copenhagen, Denmark

ISBN 978-3-030-98068-9   ISBN 978-3-030-98069-6 (eBook)
https://doi.org/10.1007/978-3-030-98069-6

© The Author(s), under exclusive license to Springer Nature Switzerland AG 2022
This work is subject to copyright. All rights are solely and exclusively licensed by the Publisher, whether the whole or part of the material is concerned, specifically the rights of translation, reprinting, reuse of illustrations, recitation, broadcasting, reproduction on microfilms or in any other physical way, and transmission or information storage and retrieval, electronic adaptation, computer software, or by similar or dissimilar methodology now known or hereafter developed.
The use of general descriptive names, registered names, trademarks, service marks, etc. in this publication does not imply, even in the absence of a specific statement, that such names are exempt from the relevant protective laws and regulations and therefore free for general use.
The publisher, the authors and the editors are safe to assume that the advice and information in this book are believed to be true and accurate at the date of publication. Neither the publisher nor the authors or the editors give a warranty, expressed or implied, with respect to the material contained herein or for any errors or omissions that may have been made. The publisher remains neutral with regard to jurisdictional claims in published maps and institutional affiliations.

Cover illustration: © Melisa Hasan

This Palgrave Macmillan imprint is published by the registered company Springer Nature Switzerland AG
The registered company address is: Gewerbestrasse 11, 6330 Cham, Switzerland

Preface

With decentralisation and digitalisation, the energy transition in electricity grids has reached the distribution level. While there continue to be many pressing issues at the transmission level, the effects and challenges at the distribution level become ever more tangible. Over the last few years, we have been working on various topics concerning economic, regulation, and operation of electricity distribution grids at the Oxford Institute for Energy Studies (OIES). We have published journal articles, discussion papers, and book chapters around these topics and eventually decided to put together this book to provide a comprehensive overview of the current trends and challenges.

The book is composed of ten chapters starting with an introduction that discusses the transition of distribution grids from basic systems at the end of nineteenth century into very complex networks in the twenty-first century. It also highlights key questions that are relevant to future economic, regulation and operation of distribution grids during the energy transition era. It then goes on in Chapter 2 to discuss the operational challenges and benefits of decentralisation as well as a necessary framework to actively engaging at the distribution level. Chapter 3 subsequently looks at the evolving role of distribution system operators and emergent models of becoming more active and interacting with TSOs and network users. The book then presents mechanisms and approaches to coordinate network use and manage constraints. In this context, Chapter 4 provides an outlook on different types of network tariffs and the trends and challenges as they become more differentiated. Similar issues are discussed in Chapter 5 with regard to network access, where new concepts of restricted access affect tariffs and market design. The latter is picked up in Chapter 6, which gives an overview of trends and developments concerning flexibility markets, presenting different designs and scopes of trading flexible network use. Next, the book broadens its perspective to energy systems integration. Chapter 7 explores the links of electricity distribution to energy efficiency, mobility, and heating demands and their potential challenges for and benefits to active distribution grids. Subsequently, Chapter 8 discusses potential merits and also limits of sector unbundling, which is widely implemented at the transmission level, in the context of future distribution grids. Chapter 9 rounds up with an assessment of the regulation of distribution grids, reviewing the options to enable the institutional and technological innovations discussed in the previous chapters in view of regulatory goals such as consumer protection and revenue sufficiency. Lastly, Chapter 10 closes with a summary and concluding remarks.

The book is written with the objective of being an informative source about electricity distribution grids for students, academics, policymakers, industry experts, and interested readers by providing a short but broad and widely accessible analysis of recent developments and future perspectives in the industry. By reading this book, the reader can expect to learn how electricity distribution grids have developed to date, what the key issues and trends are for distribution grids during the transition era and challenges for the future. The book can be part of the reading list in a course on electricity grids of the future or sustainable energy systems or alternatively a course on wider energy economics. Although the book offers a coherent story from the beginning to the end, readers can directly refer to chapters they are interested in without the need of reading the whole book. Along with being parts of a bigger picture, each chapter provides a self-contained analysis of its topic.

We would like to thank our friends, colleagues, and especially our families for their support and encouragement during this journey. The book was written during the Covid-19 pandemic which we were mainly working from home. Thus, we are very grateful for our families' support and are hopeful that the contribution this book makes to debate about on the future of distribution grids, might at least partially make up for the lost time with our families while we were focusing on the project. Also, we would like to extend our gratitude to editors at Palgrave Macmillan who supported the publication of our work.

Oxford, UK

Rahmatallah Poudineh
Christine Brandstätt
Farhad Billimoria

Contents

1 **Introduction** 1
  1.1 Evolution of the Power Distribution 2
  1.2 The Rise of Renewables and Distributed Energy Resources 4
  References 8

2 **Electricity Distribution Networks and Decentralisation Paradigm** 9
  2.1 The Paradigm of Decentralisation 10
  2.2 From Passive to Active Resources and the Challenges of Operational Security 13
  2.3 The Bumpy Road of Implementation and the Need for a Flexible Framework 18
  2.4 Conclusions 20
  References 21

3 **Evolving Roles in Distribution Networks: Resource Coordination and Control Under the Emergence of the Distribution System Operator** 25
  3.1 Introduction 26
  3.2 Operator Roles and Functionalities 27
  3.3 Power System Requirements 29
  3.4 Visibility, Predictability, and Controllability of DER-Rich Grids 30

	3.5 *Operating in a P2P Context*	34
	3.6 *DSO Operating Models*	35
	3.7 *Conclusions and Policy Implications*	37
	References	38
4	**Regulated Charges for Access to and Utilisation of Networks**	45
	4.1 *Introduction*	46
	4.2 *Tariff Schemes*	48
	4.3 *Challenges and Trends in Network Access in the Presence of Decentralisation and Decarbonisation*	53
	4.4 *Conclusions*	58
	References	59
5	**Improving Efficiency: Flexible Network Access Regime and Auction for Allocation of Network Capacity**	61
	5.1 *Introduction*	62
	5.2 *Forms of Access*	64
	5.3 *Allocation of Access*	67
	5.4 *Challenges and Trends*	71
	5.5 *Conclusion*	75
	References	76
6	**Local Markets for Decentralised Flexibility Services**	79
	6.1 *Introduction*	80
	6.2 *Market and Product Design for Flexibility*	82
	6.3 *Challenges of Market-Based Flexibility Procurement*	85
	6.4 *Conclusion*	88
	References	89
7	**Electricity Distribution Networks in the Context of Energy System Integration**	91
	7.1 *Introduction*	92
	7.2 *Multi-energy Distributed Systems*	93
	7.3 *Policy Implications and Conclusions*	96
	References	97
8	**Unbundling in Electricity Distribution Networks**	101
	8.1 *Introduction*	102

	8.2	Economics of Unbundling	103
		8.2.1 Unbundling Options for Distribution Networks	105
	8.3	Unbundling Effect on the Growth of DERs, Retail Market Competition, and Network Service Quality	108
	8.4	Information and Data Management in the Era of Decentralisation and Digitalisation	111
	8.5	Conclusions	113
		References	114
9	**Economic Regulation of Electricity Distribution Networks**		117
	9.1	Introduction	118
	9.2	Traditional Regulatory Models of Electricity Distribution Networks	119
	9.3	Digitalisation, Decentralisation, and Decarbonisation and Their Implications for Regulation of Electricity Networks	123
	9.4	New Thinking in the Regulation of Electricity Distribution Networks	125
	9.5	Conclusions	128
		References	130
10	**Conclusions**		133
	10.1	Conclusions and Policy Implications	133
Index			139

About the Authors

Rahmatallah Poudineh is senior research fellow and director of research for electricity programme at the Oxford Institute for Energy Studies. He is an engineer and economist by training and has published numerous peer-reviewed academic articles on issues related to the design of markets and regulations for future decarbonised energy systems.

Christine Brandstätt is an assistant professor with the Copenhagen School of Energy Infrastructure at Copenhagen Business School and a visiting research fellow at the Oxford Institute for Energy Studies. Her main research interests are network regulation and market design. Her recent work focusses on network pricing and energy sector integration.

Farhad Billimoria is currently a Energy Systems researcher in the Energy & Power Group at University of Oxford, and a Visiting Research Fellow at the Oxford Institute of Energy Studies. He has previously served at the Australian Energy Market Operator focusing on market design, power system security, and demand response and has over 18 years of executive experience in international energy and infrastructure financing, markets and operations.

Abbreviations

AC	Alternating Current
ACER	Agency for the Cooperation of Energy Regulators
AEMO	Australian Energy Market Operator
CAISO	California Independent System Operator
CAPEX	Capital Expenditures
CEER	Council of European Energy Regulators
CIP	Common Information Platform
DC	Direct Current
DER	Distributed Energy Resource
DERM	Distributed Energy Resource Manager
DG	Distributed Generation/Distributed Generator
DLMP	Distribution Locational Marginal Price
DNO	Distribution Network Operator
DSO	Distribution System Operator
EC	European Commission
EII	Edison Electric Institute
ESO	Electricity System Operator
EU	European Union
EV	Electric Vehicles
FACTS	Flexible Alternating Current Transmission System
FCAS	Frequency Control Ancillary Services
GCC	Gulf Cooperation Council
GENCO	Generation Company
HV	High Voltage
ICT	Information and Communications Technology
IDSO	Independent Distribution System Operator

ISO	Independent System Operator
kW	Kilowatt
kWh	Kilowatt-hour
LCOE	Levelized Cost of Electricity
LDV	Light Duty Vehicles
LMP	Locational Marginal Price
LV	Low Voltage
MC	Marginal Cost
MV	Medium Voltage
NEM	National Electricity Market
NGESO	National Grid Electricity System Operator
OPEX	Operating Expenditures
OPF	Optimal Power Flow
P2P	Peer-to-peer
PJM	Pennsylvania, New Jersey, Maryland System Operator
PV	Photovoltaic
RTO	Regional Transmission Operator
SCADA	Supervisory Control and Data Acquisition
SCED	Security Constrained Economic Dispatch
TO	Transmission Owner
TOTEX	Total Expenditure approach
TSO	Transmission System Operator
US	United States of America
V2G	Vehicle-to-grid
VPP	Virtual Power Plant
VSM	Virtual Synchronous Machine

List of Figures

Fig. 4.1	Netting injection and withdrawal for prosumers (*Source* authors based on Brandstätt [2021a])	52
Fig. 8.1	The spectrum of unbundling models in the electricity transmission network (*Source* authors)	106
Fig. 8.2	Three options for the structure of the electricity distribution sector (*Source* authors)	106

CHAPTER 1

Introduction

Abstract The rise of renewable and distributed energy sources has resulted in a fundamental change in the way in which electricity is traditionally produced, distributed, and sold. Centralised power generation is increasingly giving way to a decentralised paradigm as new technologies continue to allow for different forms of electricity generation, storage, distribution, and trade. Electricity distribution networks are at the heart of this transformation which means that these networks will be highly affected by current trends. This chapter briefly reviews the evolution of power distribution and argues that the rise of decentralisation calls into question the traditional economic, regulation, and operation of distribution grids.

Keywords Power distribution history · Centralised generation · Decentralisation · Distributed energy resources (DERs)

1.1 Evolution of the Power Distribution

In 1882, the first US electricity distribution system was built by Thomas Edison which carried electrical energy from Pearl Street power station to a few customers within and around one mile square (Electricity Distribution—IER, 2021). Although this was a small operation compared to electricity distribution networks of today, it was the US's first electricity grid which means many of the grid components were invented and used for the first time (Earlier in the same year, Edison had opened a similar system in London).

Edison's electricity distribution system was considered revolutionary as it was the first time in history that energy user was separated from energy source and all the inconveniences that are associated with it. This is aside from the fact that with light bulbs replacing candles and burning lamps, the whole experience of lighting became cleaner, safer, and more pleasant for end users (ibid).

During the twentieth century, electricity distribution networks evolved technologically into complex systems consisting of distribution substations,[1] distribution transformers,[2] and all the interconnecting lines in between (Poudineh et al., 2017). The common configuration model for the distribution grid, especially in low-load density areas, was a radical approach in which consumers have a connection to only one primary feeder. This mode of operation was widespread mainly because of its simplicity, the ease of coordinating protection devices on the grid, and most importantly, the cost. The alternative approach is a loop system in which end users are connected to two primary feeders in a closed loop. In this model, consumers enjoy a higher level of reliability because when one section fails or is out of service, customers can be served by the other feeder.

As electricity networks expanded, an important challenge was the control and operation of such extensive systems. Although automated remote sensing and control are less common in distribution grids compared with that in transmission networks, distribution lines which are located at the upstream of the primary feeders are monitored

---

[1] These are equipment that step down the voltage level between the transmission grid and primary feeders (i.e., the primary supply line that connects to secondary networks).

[2] Transformers further lowers the voltage between the primary feeders and end users' premise connection.

and controlled via Supervisory Control and Data Acquisition (SCADA) systems (Poudineh et al., 2017). Due to high number of distribution transformers and connected users, the monitoring of individual distribution network equipment is usually economically inefficient. Thus, most of the time, distribution network operators are notified of outages through a customer's call and the process of locating and restoring the fault is often manual and lengthy. Overall, during much of the last century, the main direction of technological development in the distribution network was in improving distribution lines monitoring, control, and data processing/automation.

Similar to the grid technology that was improving during the last century, the governance and market structure of the electricity sector were evolving too. Historically, distribution networks along with the entire supply chain were part of an integrated monopoly which was mainly private during the first half of the twentieth century especially in industrial economies. After the second world war, these infrastructures became nationalised in many of the industrialised countries in order to facilitate investment as electricity was considered a strategic sector for economic recovery.

At the end of the 1980s, a trend started across the globe, pioneered by countries such as Chile, England, and Norway, to liberalise the electricity sector. Different countries followed different paths in the liberalisation process, but the essence of this process entailed separation of the network business, as a natural monopoly, from generation and retail supply which are potentially competitive. In this way, transmission and distribution networks became regulated natural monopoly companies with the mandate of being neutral market facilitators. Much of the regulatory effort at this stage was focused on incentivising cost efficiency, service quality improvement, and a fair and efficient networks access regime.

The liberalisation and privatisation of the electricity sector happened in a context that this industry has traditionally relied on economies of scale to provide electricity to its customers (Li, 2020). By the middle of the twentieth century, the optimum size of thermal power plants had already increased from a few tens of MW to several hundreds of MW with a significant impact on reducing the cost of utilities. As a result, the electricity supply industry evolved into a centralised top-down structure that remained almost unchanged during much of the last century.

1.2 The Rise of Renewables and Distributed Energy Resources

Since the turn of the new century, with the rise of decarbonisation objectives on the agenda of policymakers and introduction of extensive direct and indirect subsidies for low-carbon technologies, the operating environment of electricity networks started to change. The cost of alternative generation technologies such as solar and wind power started to decline. In the second decade of the new millennium, the industry witnessed a massive cost decline for renewable energy technologies some of which, such as onshore wind, are already among the cheapest methods of generating electricity (IRENA, 2021).

This cost decline was not just for utility-scale renewable energy resources. Indeed, smaller distributed resources such as rooftop solar PV have also experienced a similar cost fall. The levelised cost of electricity (LCOE) for rooftop solar PV in countries such as Australia, Japan, Italy, US, and Germany have declined from between USD 0.304/kWh and USD 0.460/kWh in 2010 to between USD 0.055/kWh and USD 0.236/kWh in 2020 which translates into a cost decline between 49 and 82% (IRENA, 2021). A similar trend can also be seen for battery storage both at the level of utility scale and residential scale. According to IRENA (2017), the total cost of small-scale lithium-ion batteries in Germany has fallen by 60% between 2014 and 2017. It is also expected that battery installations for stationary applications see another 54–61% cost decline by 2030 (IRENA, 2017).

The cost decline of renewable energy resources along with a range of government incentives have resulted in a rapid growth of decentralisation in some regions. A pioneering example in this regard is Australia. It is forecasted that by 2035, around 33% of generation capacity in this country will be behind the meter (i.e., onsite or on the energy user's side of the meter) (Macquarie.com., 2021). This number is 18% for Japan, 17% for Germany, 15% for Europe, and 10% for the US within the same period (ibid). These show that there is an overall trend towards further decentralisation in the electricity sector as distributed energy resources (DERs) grow. DERs are flexible resources that are connected to low-voltage distribution network and capable of producing electricity or managing demand. These include, for example, rooftop solar PV, solar water heating, stationary home batteries, electric vehicles (EVs), vehicle to grid (V2G), demand response, energy efficiency, and home energy management systems.

DERs provide benefit to the power system such as avoided infrastructure investment, lowering carbon emissions, and increased resilience. By reducing the need for bulk power generation, DERs not only provide energy value but also lower transmission and distribution network losses which mean lower costs to consumers. Additionally, depending on DERs utilisation during the system peak hours, these resources can provide system-level capacity benefits by lowering the need for investment in generation and transmission capacity. Similarly, DERs can defer investment in distribution network assets if they are incentivised to operate during the local peak hours. Finally, DERs can provide a range of important ancillary services such as operating reserve and frequency response which are increasingly becoming scarce as traditional thermal generation are either retired, displaced, or phased out.

However, the growth of DERs has technical and economic implications for both distribution network utilities and the bulk power system. From a technical perspective, DERs often generate electricity as direct current (DC) which needs to be converted to alternating current (AC) through inverters before they can be injected into the grid or used by the owner. Inverter-based grid connection introduces its own challenges related to voltage, power quality, and protection system coordination at the distribution network level. Higher levels of DERs penetration also require a more effective coordination mechanism between distribution and transmission network operators in order to address reverse power flow and associated operational complexities (Horowitz et al., 2019).

From an economic perspective, DERs complicate the task of allocating network capacity and setting grid tariffs. First, historically, distribution grid tariffs are not designed to account for DERs which means penetration of these resources may lead to network congestion and capacity constraints. For example, excessive injections of rooftop solar PVs into the distribution grid or EVs random charging can easily overload the low-voltage network. Furthermore, efficient long-term planning of distribution and transmission networks require an accurate forecast of DERs penetration something which is traditionally overlooked. Under-forecasting the growth of DERs can lead to unnecessary investment in the bulk generation resources and associated infrastructure with consequences of putting rate payers or developers at the risk of bearing inefficiently high costs. Similarly, over forecasting of DERs can result in lower than necessary investment in generation and network infrastructures with implications for the reliability of electricity supply.

Apart from decentralisation and growth of DERs, the operating environment of electricity distribution networks is also affected by wider digitalisation trend across the economy. The areas such as service platforms, smart devices, cloud, and advanced analytics are emerging which enable utility companies to create value by increasing asset life cycle of energy infrastructure, optimising electricity network flow, and offering customer-centric products. The emergence of new business models such as aggregators, energy as a service as well as new forms of trading such as peer-to-peer models are also, to a great extent, driven by digitalisation growth in the energy sector and across the whole economy.

These developments call into question the traditional economic, regulation, and operation of distribution network utilities. There is now debate among experts about the future role of distribution system operators as the growth of DERs increasingly require these networks to take on a more active role like that of the transmission system operator. There are also a range of other important questions such as: how to best allocate limited network capacity given the rise of variable generation and demand, how to create distribution-led markets to utilise flexibility of DERs to benefit the system and end users, how the decentralised energy paradigm fits within the context of the broader energy system integration, what are options for unbundling at the distribution network level, and how best to regulate distribution network companies during the energy transition era. This book tries to address these issues in a concise and informative manner.

The outline of this book is as follows. The next chapter covers the market and operational context for increasing levels of decentralisation, and the challenges and opportunities presented by an increasingly decentralised grid. Chapter 3 focuses upon emergent models of operation and coordination of decentralised energy resources. The chapter covers the roles played by distribution utilities and operators, in moving from passive network operator roles to an increasingly active scheduler and coordinator of distributed resources, to a platform provider.

Chapter 4 introduces the concept of regulated charges as means both to finance the infrastructure as well as to coordinate network users. It covers the traditional distinction of one-off charges for connection and continuous charges for network usage. The chapter also reviews issues of cost incidence, on feed-in versus withdrawal as well practical simplifications such as energy netting and approximations for usage of the infrastructure. Chapter 5, on the other hand, looks at the efficient allocation of access to existing and future grid capacity. The analysis departs from the concept of restricted rather than universal network access and discusses the possibility of assigning access rights via auctions as opposed to offering them at regulated prices.

Chapter 6 provides an overview of different concepts for local and decentralised markets for flexibility. It distinguishes between network operators' need for flexibility to manage scarcity and capacity development and a corresponding market demand for flexibility to balance supply portfolios. The chapter also discusses flexibility markets in relation to traditional mechanisms for flexibility in the form of balancing, redispatch, and curtailment regimes.

Chapter 7 examines how the decentralised energy paradigm fits within the context of the broader energy system transition. In particular, it covers the relationship between decentralisation and the following three energy system integration themes (i) the electrification of mobility and transport, (ii) buildings and energy efficiency, and (iii) multi-energy systems and decarbonisation of heat. At the end, the chapter will provide a vision of a future integrated decentralised energy system and a market and operational roadmap to reach this objective.

Chapter 8 evaluates advantages and disadvantages of unbundling at distribution networks. It argues that although the debate about unbundling of transmission networks is very well established in the post-liberalisation era, the discussion at the distribution level is not straightforward. This is because distribution networks are significantly more complex than transmission networks which means that the rules and regulation of bulk power and transmission system may not be directly applicable to the distribution system.

Chapter 9 discusses the need for a new regulatory model in electricity distribution networks. It argues that the transition of electricity systems has implications for the way costs and incentive for electricity networks are determined. During the energy transition, a key objective of economic incentives is to align the operation of the network with wider decarbonisation objectives. This is to encourage the network utilities to create value for society by engaging in activities that facilitate the whole system optimisation and maximises the value of the network.

Finally, Chapter 10 provides the concluding remarks.

References

Horowitz, K. A., Peterson, Z., Coddington, M. H., Ding, F., Sigrin, B. O., Saleem, D., Baldwin, S. E., Lydic, B., Stanfield, S. C., Enbar, N., Coley, S., Sundararajan, A., & Schroeder, C. (2019, April). *An overview of Distributed Energy Resource (DER) interconnection: Current practices and emerging solutions*. Technical Report, National Renewable Energy Lab. (NREL).

IER. (2021). *Electricity Distribution—IER*. Institute for Energy Research. [online]. https://www.instituteforenergyresearch.org/electricity-distribution/. Accessed 6 September 2021.

IRENA. (2017). *Electricity storage and renewables: Costs and markets to 2030*, International Renewable Energy Agency.

IRENA. (2021). *Renewable power generation costs in 2020*. International Renewable Energy Agency.

Li, F. (2020, September). *The future structure of the electrical supply system—From economies of scale to economies of flexibility* (Issue 124). Oxford Energy Forum.

Macquarie.com. (2021). *Australia points the way to a decentralised energy future|Macquarie Group*. [online]. https://www.macquarie.com/au/en/perspectives/australia-points-the-way-to-a-decentralised-energy-future.html. Accessed 21 September 2021.

Poudineh, R., Peng, D., & Mirnezami, S. R (2017). *Electricity networks: Technology, future role and economic incentives for innovation*. Oxford Institute for Energy Studies. EL27.

CHAPTER 2

Electricity Distribution Networks and Decentralisation Paradigm

Abstract In this chapter we describe the paradigm shift that is currently underway in the energy system away from passive distributed energy resources towards those that are more active and dynamic and are expected to play a larger role in enabling a secure and reliable zero-carbon electricity system. It highlights some of the technical and operational challenges that arise from transitioning away from a predominantly centralised, synchronous power system along with the new opportunities that arise from advanced inverter technology development. As the pace of change required by socio-political and environmental objectives may make the system more susceptible to operational vulnerabilities it is proposed that a comprehensive risk management framework accompany the DER policy transition, recognising the potentially 'bumpy' nature of electricity transition.

Keywords Electricity distribution · Decentralisation · Distributed energy resources · Prosumer · Distributed markets.

2.1 The Paradigm of Decentralisation

An hour north of the British port city of Newcastle, just outside the town of Rothbury in Northumberland, England lies a 1,700-acre sprawling country estate known as 'Cragside'. Described by the contemporary Victorian magazine The World Truly as 'the palace of a modern magician' the manor housed guests including the Shah of Persia, the King of Siam, and King Edward VII (Irlam, 1988). The owner of the estate, Lord William Armstrong, was an eminent scientist, inventor, and philanthropist. In a varied but highly successful career he developed the first effective hydraulic systems and made major innovations in armaments manufacture and defence systems. Armstrong was also an early and avid user of electricity. In 1870, a Siemens Dynamo was installed at the base of an existing dam and pump house and connected to the manor and farm buildings. This made Cragside the first house in the world to be lit by hydroelectric power, and its patrons the world's first 'prosumers' of electricity.[1]

Indeed, the early development of the electricity industry itself had a very strong distributed flavour to it with the first commercial electricity generation plants serving only areas encompassing a few city blocks. Edison's Pearl Street station was one in a group of distributed DC power stations all around New York City, serving a variety of local commercial customers (Sulzberger, 2003). The first Niagara Falls hydro power station developed by German entrepreneur Jacob Schoellkopf in 1882, was also constructed with the intent of being one in a group of small, distributed resources powering a community-based energy system. Over time the growth of small distributed systems gave way to larger centralised power stations, enabled by the scalability of generation technology allowing high power density generation stations and the development of AC transmission, which together enabled these polluting and noisy stations away to be located away from its consumers. The centralisation of electric power eventually became a mainstay of the industry marking a sojourn for the deployment and prospects of distributed electricity resources, that is until more recent times.

Moving forward one hundred and fifty years from Armstrong's original turbine installation, we have observed a renaissance in the prospects

---

[1] *The term prosumer, coined by futurist Alvin Toffler in 1980, is an agent that both consume and produces, and in the energy context* (Parag & Sovacool, 2016).

for distributed energy resources in a modern electric grid. This initially came in the form of rooftop solar photovoltaic (PV) installations 'behind the meter' at residential and commercial consumer premises. The drivers of take-up were diverse and included policy incentives and support, technology cost reductions, efficiency advancements coupled with motivations for tariff avoidance, and environmental awareness (Chapman et al., 2016; Sommerfeld et al., 2017). Taken together these factors fueled a boom in the deployment of distributed resources in many grids that continues to this day. In 2018, distributed PV additions accounted for 40% of total PV growth worldwide and exceeded the net capacity additions of coal and nuclear combined (IEA, 2020). Globally, rooftop solar generating capacity is estimated at 107 GW in 2020, of which 19 GW is residential scale and going forward is expected to reach 160 GW by 2022.

Certain grids have already begun preparing for scenarios where most of the electricity across the grid could be supplied by distributed resources. In Australia, where 1 in 4 addressable households currently has rooftop PV installed making up 14% of total capacity in the National Electricity Market (NEM), the Australian Energy Market Operator (AEMO) expects consumer-owned generation capacity could triple (under a steady progress or slow change scenario) or quadruple (under a fast change scenario) by 2040 (AEMO, 2021a). Indeed, given the level of distributed generation South Australia in particular is already at negative operational demand (which is electricity consumption demand net off rooftop PV generation) introducing a new array of operational challenges for the system. In the UK, the Future Energy Scenarios projected by the National Grid Electricity System Operator (NGESO) expects distributed sources of energy to range from 22–31% of peak demand by 2030. In California, rooftop solar capacity is estimated at just under 10 GW (CAISO, 2021). With the electricity mix in the state required to be meet 100% renewables by 2040 objective, distributed energy resources (DER) are expected to play a major role in the supply mix of the future.

This distributed future presents both opportunities and challenges and requires a paradigm shift in the approach to planning, investing in, and operating electricity grids. The key challenges in enabling large-scale DER deployment are related to operational security (integration, operational security, and reliability and grid codes), markets and coordination (distributed-wholesale interface, dispatch, and pricing), network management, and socio-economic considerations (such as relating to privacy, data, and equity). On the positive side, DER also presents opportunity to harness load flexibility and distributed resiliency as part of a suite of solutions to manage a grid that is increasingly dominated by variable and uncertain forms of generation. DER has the potential to add significant value in relation to improving the reliability, resiliency, and security of the grid and can provide a range of benefits including the reduction of electricity supply and transmission costs, improved balancing of load with generation, deferral or cancellation of network augmentation, provision of system services, resiliency enhancement, and retail tariff reduction. Properly implemented this could enable the development of a true two-sided electricity market fulfilling the original vision and aspiration of the original Schweppian electricity market design (Schweppe, 1978).

The research in the distributed energy resources space is rich and varies by focus and scope, and correspondingly the nomenclature is varied too. As such, before delving into the substantive content of this book, it is important to clarify the focus of this book as it relates to the definition of DER within the literature.

What defines a DER from other resources in the electricity grid? An early framing of the definition of DER by Ackerman, which continues to have relevance today, identified a range of factors most relevant to distinguishing distributed resources (termed distributed generation in the earlier nomenclature) (Ackermann et al., 2001). One of the factors most relevant to distinguishing DER from other resources in the grid is the location of the resource. What may seem an obvious but nevertheless critical distinction is the location of DER being within the distribution grid as opposed to being connected to the transmission network. Some works seek to narrow the concept further to resources located at customer sites. This distinction has been brought into enhanced relevance given the emergence of rooftop PV technology and the energy prosumer. For our purposes we will maintain the focus on assets and resources located within the distribution grid through certain issues, such as network pricing and resource coordination have relevance to behind-the-meter resources and we will clarify such application in these cases. Resource type is also a potential differentiator. Much of the deployment of DER in the last decade has been in the form of distributed generation (such as rooftop PV). Going forward, however, a wider and larger array of resources have the potential to impact the consumption and generation at the customer site. This includes distributed storage and electric vehicles, but also a range of energy monitoring, control and communication systems that enable demand-side energy management and demand response. Thus, given the potential for these resources to impact the planning and operation of the electricity grid, it is important not to exclude them from consideration when thinking about critical issues such as electricity pricing, network access and operation. Furthermore, the technology space under consideration with respect to DER ranges from recent power electronic-based technology such as solar PV and battery storage, but also includes a range of fossil fuel and hybrid fossil/renewable resources. Our focus in this book will be on the former, but noting the interactions with existing conventional fossil resources especially under transition. Under the definitional framework, scale was not considered a highly relevant factor in distinguishing DER from other resources. Nevertheless, we are primarily focused in this book on smaller-scale resources that tend to be deployed within the distribution grid. For example, a large utility-scale wind farm connected to the distribution grid, which is treated for all main intents and purposes as a wholesale electricity market asset is of less relevance to the focus of this book. Finally, while the focus of this work is not centred upon microgrids, nano-grids, or embedded resources, where relevant we will mention particular issues relating to such forms of participation as relevant.

2.2 From Passive to Active Resources and the Challenges of Operational Security

In this section, we seek to highlight how technology advancement has enabled a shift in the DER participation model from relatively static 'set-and-forget' resources to active and responsive resources that can be controlled or coordinated at multiple levels of hierarchy. We highlight potential operational and coordination risks and opportunities emerging from a transition to more dynamic resources, and the need for more careful consideration of security and grid implications.

The deployment of DER in the modern era has been epitomised by the growth of rooftop solar PV panels, typically installed on residential rooftops, begin and in late 1990s and early 2000s, with capacity growth reaching extraordinary rates during the 2010s and still strong today. These solar systems typically comprised the solar generation system, which is a set of panels and associated housing/mounting/racking, connected to a DC/AC inverter which connected into the consumer's grid connection. The inverter forms the primary interface between the DC generation system, and what was (and at the time of writing still is) a predominantly 'synchronous' AC grid (Kroposki et al., 2017).[2] To convert DC energy into grid-compatible AC energy, inverter's control systems have traditionally relied upon voltage phase measurements from the grid itself to effectively synchronise with the grid's waveform. This is known as a 'grid-following' inverter system. In a situation where inverters were the minority of the grid and the grid's existing voltage waveform was strong, this was an acceptable approach to interface to the grid. Other important technical parameters for the systems included trip settings, i.e., the frequency and voltages at which inverter systems are set to trip off, thereby disconnecting the solar system from the grid and anti-islanding—which ensures that the system trips off during times of grid outage. In the absence of storage or other control systems to balance the generation and consumption of power at the consumer site, these systems could not function independently (as an island) and hence were required to trip when the grid itself was not in service. The relevance of such technical settings is enhanced as we shift from a grid that was predominantly synchronous to one which is expected to be dominated by inverter-based resources in the not-too-distant future. Overall, however early vintage these systems were designed to be relatively passive systems—they generated power when the weather resources were available and the grid interface was stable and strong enough to enable the injection of power into the system and tripped or temporarily terminated operations when the grid interface was unstable, such as during frequency or voltage dips.

The operational challenges associated with a new power electronics interface are currently being observed across many large-scale power systems around the world. Two critical issues relate to (i) inertia and frequency management and (ii) system strength and voltage management (Billimoria et al., 2020). First, the inertia stored in the spinning mass of synchronous turbines have traditionally provided a buffer to the system in the event of frequency disturbances. Inverter-based resource (IBR) by virtue of being connected via power electronics do not have the same natural inertial response, and thus in an inverter-dominated grid the loss

---

[2] While the above describes a typical solar system, we also note that there have been deployments of other forms of distributed generation including wind. The overall setup of such systems is similar, in that it flows from a generation system (in this case wind turbines) connected to an inverter or group of inverters (depending upon scale) with similar interface settings and challenges as noted above.

of synchronous inertia means the operational management of frequency is more challenging (Badesa et al., 2020). Second, synchronous generation naturally injects high levels of current into the system in the event of a fault, which serves to abate voltage degradation and enhance recovery of voltage to steady state levels (Keller & Kroposki, 2010). Not only are grid-following inverters unable to provide such services, but they also rely upon a strong grid and stable phasor measurements to synchronise with the grid. As grids shift towards a resource mix that is increasingly dominated by inverter-based resources, parts of the grid are becoming increasingly weak resulting in risks relating to potential maloperation of protection systems and instability in inverter control and response (Mancarella & Billimoria, 2021). In general, these technical risks are not unique to DER, and apply to all resources that use inverter technology to connect with the grid including grid and network scale resources. However, the decentralised and heterogenous nature of DER does pose a set of unique challenges related to operational management and technical mitigation.

In Australia, a recent study by AEMO on the impacts of power system disturbances on DER found 'considerable evidence of extensive disconnection of DER in response to voltage disturbances'—measuring up to 50% on average of units located within 50 km of the fault location and with up to 20% greater than 250 km away. Moreover, the inconsistency of disconnection is also relevant especially for sites at greater distances from the fault location, ranging for example from 5% to ~ 45% for units 150–250 km away. The loss of DER generation can increase contingency sizes and impact the market through interventions such as the enablement of increased frequency reserves, or network constraints. The inconsistency of response creates uncertainty in anticipating the size of the contingency and required mitigating action, and increasingly so as the size of DER penetration grows across the system. As a consequence of such risks, new grid standards now require enhanced capabilities from DER to 'ride-through' such disturbances to mitigate the size of future contingencies (Quint et al., 2019).

Since the early models, significant advancements in panel efficiency and manufacturing processes have enabled order-of-magnitude cost reductions and by consequence scaleup in the deployment of DER.[3] Yet such

---

[3] We exclude from our analysis advancement in axis tracking systems for solar, since these tend to be deployed in utility-scale systems.

changes, while improving economics of DER relative to alternatives this, on its own, did not alter the basic operating framework and participation models of DER in the market.

A combination of additional advancements in resource, control, and coordination systems and frameworks has enabled a transformation in the very nature of participation of DER in the electricity system, from a passive generator to highly controllable and configurable resources that can be aggregated to provide valuable services that enable electricity system transition (Burger & Luke, 2017). The onset of distributed storage (both in stationary and in the form of electric vehicle) enables greater flexibility in consumption and injection of energy by DER. It has also paved the way for sustained technical delivery of additional system services such as frequency control, voltage control, and congestion management. The growth of electric vehicles intricately bounds consumer and commercial transport dynamics and electricity usage, with the potential to provide further flexibility services through vehicle-to-grid (V2G) actuation (Sousa et al., 2019). Smart home and smart-appliance technology combined with real-time communication and control protocols enable flexibility and control of a wider range of consumer energy uses including heating and cooling.

This advanced flexibility expands the range of services that can be provided by distributed resources to meet both local and system-wide needs. DERs have the potential to deliver critical grid services including frequency regulation and reserves, voltage regulation and reactive reserves, system balancing and network congestion management, to the enhancement of reliability, security, and resiliency (Eid et al., 2016). The AEMO Virtual Power Plant (VPP) Demonstrations programme was established to prove technical commercial viability for aggregated DER in the form of VPPs to respond to power system events and provide frequency control ancillary services (FCAS) to maintain power system security (AEMO, 2021b). The project was able to successfully demonstrate both the technical participation of DER in FCAS markets, but also the capability to generate sustained revenue from market participation. In the UK, the Power Potential trial is being implemented by the National Grid Electricity System Operator (NGESO) and UK Power Networks, the largest Distribution Network Operator (DNO) in the UK. Power Potential seeks to contract with DER for the provision of reactive and active power services in the southern region of Great Britain using a competitive mechanism (Anaya & Pollitt, 2020). In recent years the Californian grid has been plagued by extreme heatwaves and bushfires, events which are expected to become more common given undeniable evidence of global warming and climate change (IPCC, 2021). In a new virtual power plant scheme, Tesla will let Californian owners of its Powerwall battery feed electricity back into the power grid during periods of high energy demand to prevent blackouts in the state (Weaver, 2021). Scheme participants will receive a push notification on their devices during periods when system operator requires flexibility (CAISO Flex Alerts).

Motivated by the challenges of inverters that are reliant upon a strong grid, designs are developing for grid-forming controls for power inverters devised so they can operate autonomously, without relying on synchronous generation. Grid-forming inverters are those that do not rely upon measurements of grid phase angle to synchronise with the grid. While the term 'grid-forming' is applied to range of control loop designs, including droop-control, virtual oscillator, and virtual synchronous machine (VSM) models they share a common objective of allowing self-sustaining inverter interfaces, thereby enabling grid operability with an inverter-dominated grid (Lasseter et al., 2020). These technologies have been in trials in recent years (Lasseter et al., 2020), but are now being deployed in scale in large power systems including the National Electricity Market of Australia (Parkinson, 2021). While to date this implementation has been focused upon utility-scale storage, this technology could also be extended to DER in the future.

While the additional flexibility of DER offers an enhanced range services to meet the needs of a decarbonised electricity system, it also presents a range of operational risks that need to be managed. Patterns of use may be less predictable with the potential for increasingly heterogenous behaviour as between system, local, and individual uses, and as between different forms of market and system participation. Different control systems and system specifications also present potentials for different fault and disturbance response, making system reserving and contingency planning more complex. A balance needs to be struck between (i) setting the baseline specification for DER through grid standards, (ii) enabling a wider and enhanced range of participation from DER, and (iii) sourcing reserves and contingency services from the grid to manage the emergent operational challenges. This will require close and ongoing coordination and engagement between critical stakeholders including the planners, policymakers, operators, and consumers.

2.3 The Bumpy Road of Implementation and the Need for a Flexible Framework

In 1978, the late MIT Professor Fred Schweppe published an article called 'Power systems "2000": hierarchical control strategies' which paints a surprisingly precise view of the electricity future (Schweppe, 1978). The future predicted by Schweppe envisioned (i) the introduction of more customer generation and/or energy storage, (ii) greatly increased weather dependance, (iii) hierarchical control and customer level actuation, and (iv) an energy marketplace that allows customers and utilities to trade as equals. Today each of these themes thread through commonly espoused visions of a 'two-way' dynamic and consumer-centric future grid (Bose & Low, 2019).

While we already have observed the rise of customer level resources and some level of weather dependency, the full achievement of Schweppe's vision will depend upon a successful implementation of the passive to the active deployment and actuation of DER, which remains subject to the resolution of some of the matters that form the remaining chapters of this book. Included in this list are (i) the selection of co-ordination strategies[4] for DER in a manner that maintains operational reliability and security of the grid, closely linked with (ii) the functional allocation of coordination roles across the distribution system—from network operator, system operator, and market operator/scheduler (ii) network access and rates in an environment of increasingly active and heterogenous DER, where prior transmission network (iii) unbundling of ownership and of functionality in distribution networks (iv) market and pricing designs for active DER engagement in the system (v) network regulation in distributed networks and (vi) the integration of DER in a wider multi-energy system incorporating the electrification of mobility and heat.

The next phase of DER integration is likely to be a highly complex and intricate one. From an economic and technical viewpoint new thinking on the problem will be required. The engineering is complicated, and in many cases the technical understanding of newly observed system phenomena is still evolving (especially in relation to operational security). Moreover, while the pace of technology advancement is rapid, the

---

[4] Coordination strategies for DER vary across a taxonomy of direct control and indirect control, of which the latter can be further segregated into mediated coordination, bilateral coordination and implicit coordination (Charbonnier, 2022).

enablement of such technologies requires standardisation at some level (such as for example in the definition of services). Thus, the development of technical standards and specifications is required to proceed apace. The economics is similarly complex, and many of the concepts, such as locational marginal pricing (LMP), economic dispatch, and unbundling, that are common in a transmission network context may not directly translate over to the distribution grid context for a variety of reasons including computational tractability, system element visibility and predictability, data shareability and privacy, and the political economy of direct consumer-level engagement.

Moreover, given broader environmental policy and political imperatives, integration will likely need to proceed a record pace of change (Bogdanov et al., 2021). This is likely to be driven by a push for broader electricity system decarbonisation and the importance placed by policymakers on DER as an enabler of such. While it may be tempting to seek to slow the pace of change—for example to better quantify system security implications or to agree with technical standards, it is not clear that such delays will even be viable in a socio-political context.

Change at such a pace is likely to present risks to the operability of the system and could make the power system more fragile (Mancarella & Billimoria, 2021). Waiting for standards and technical issues to be resolved is likely to be difficult given the impetus for the facilitation of DER. On the other hand, moving forward to implementation and deployment without an appreciation of operational implications could risk the security of the grid and the technical and engineering assurance in the DER pathway. The balanced view suggests a coordinated facilitation of DER that strikes the right balance between resource enablement and operational risk mitigation.

Achieving such balance at every step of the transition may be challenging, suggesting that the road to implementation could be a bumpy one. In such an environment, it is important that along with the focus on enablement of DER there should be a comprehensive operational risk management framework that monitors the full range of risks relating to the transition (including technical, economic, and social) and develops mitigation alternatives. It also calls for a supportive regulatory and policy environment which gives market designers and operator the flexibility to respond to risks as they emerge. While it may not be possible to foresee every risk and outcome, it is critical that the relevant parties are able to monitor and respond accordingly. Finally, this also stresses the importance of flexible and modular systems development that is adaptable to technical and market understanding.

2.4 Conclusions

Over the last two decades, we observed a renaissance in the prospects for DERs in a modern electric grid. A revolution that initially came in the form of rooftop solar PV installations but later extended to other distributed technologies. The drivers of take-up are a range of factors such as policy incentives, technology cost reductions, avoiding high retail tariffs, and environmental concerns. These factors led to a boom in the deployment of DERs in many distribution grids that continues to this day. Certain grids such as in Australia, California, and the UK have already begun preparing for scenarios where most of the electricity across the grid could be supplied by distributed resources.

The growth of DERs presents both opportunities and challenges and requires a paradigm shift in the approach to planning, investing in, and operating electricity grids. Key challenges imposed by penetration of DERs are operational security and reliability of the grid, coordination between TSO and DSOs, network capacity management, and also issues related to privacy, data, and equity. At the same time, DERs can provide significant benefits such as load flexibility and distributed resiliency, reducing electricity supply and transmission costs, deferring or avoiding network augmentation, providing system services, resiliency enhancement, and retail tariff reduction.

Realising the benefits and overcoming challenges of integration of DERs require addressing several technical and regulatory issues. These include: (a) the selection of coordination strategies for DERs and the functional allocation of coordination roles across the distribution system—from network operator, system operator, and market operator/scheduler (b) addressing the issue of network access and grid capacity allocation in an environment of increasingly active and heterogenous DERs (c) rethinking unbundling in distribution networks (d) designing appropriate market and pricing for active DER engagement in the system and finally (e) introducing effective network regulation frameworks that encourage innovation and whole system optimisation by distribution system operators. The following chapters discuss these issues in more details.

References

Ackermann, T., Andersson, G., & Söder, L. (2001). Distributed generation: A definition. *Electric Power Systems Research, 57*(3), 195–204. https://doi.org/10.1016/S0378-7796(01)00101-8

AEMO. (2020). *South Australian electricity report*. https://aemo.com.au/-/media/files/electricity/nem/planning_and_forecasting/sa_advisory/2020/2020-south-australian-electricity-report.pdf?la=en

AEMO. (2021a). *2021 inputs, assumptions and scenarios report*. https://aemo.com.au/-/media/files/major-publications/isp/2021/2021-inputs-assumptions-and-scenarios-report-overview.pdf?la=en

AEMO. (2021b). *Virtual power Ppant Ddmonstrations knowledge sharing report 3*. https://arena.gov.au/assets/2021/02/aemo-virtual-power-plant-demonstrations-report-3.pdf

Anaya, K. L., & Pollitt, M. G. (2020). Reactive power procurement: A review of current trends. *Applied Energy, 270,*. https://doi.org/10.1016/J.APENERGY.2020.114939

Badesa, L., Teng, F., & Strbac, G. (2020). *Economic value of inertia in low-carbon power systems*. https://doi.org/10.1109/ISGTEurope.2017.8260153

Billimoria, F., Mancarella, P., & Poudineh, R. (2020). *Market design for system security in low-carbon electricity grids: from the physics to the economics* (Issue June). https://doi.org/10.26889/9781784671600

Bogdanov, D., Ram, M., Aghahosseini, A., Gulagi, A., Oyewo, A. S., Child, M., Caldera, U., Sadovskaia, K., Farfan, J., De Souza Noel Simas Barbosa, L., Fasihi, M., Khalili, S., Traber, T., & Breyer, C. (2021). Low-cost renewable electricity as the key driver of the global energy transition towards sustainability. *Energy, 227*, 120467. https://doi.org/10.1016/J.ENERGY.2021.120467

Bose, S., & Low, S. H. (2019). Some emerging challenges in electricity markets. In *Smart Grid Control* (pp. 29–45). Springer. https://doi.org/10.1007/978-3-319-98310-3_2

Burger, S. P., & Luke, M. (2017). Business models for distributed energy resources: A review and empirical analysis. *Energy Policy, 109*, 230–248. https://doi.org/10.1016/j.enpol.2017.07.007

CAISO. (2021). *Behind-the-meter solar impact to demand and operations*. https://www.wecc.org/Administrative/Motley-Behind-the-Meter%20Solar%20Impact%20to%20Demand%20Forecasting_February%202021.pdf

Chapman, A. J., McLellan, B., & Tezuka, T. (2016). Residential solar PV policy: An analysis of impacts, successes and failures in the Australian case. *Renewable Energy, 86*, 1265–1279. https://doi.org/10.1016/J.RENENE.2015.09.061

Charbonnier, F., Morstyn, T., & McCulloch, M. (2022). *Coordination of resources at the edge of the electricity grid: Systematic review and classification. 0362*, 0–3. https://arxiv.org/pdf/2202.03786

Eid, C., Codani, P., Perez, Y., Reneses, J., & Hakvoort, R. (2016). Managing electric flexibility from distributed energy resources: A review of incentives for market design. *Renewable and Sustainable Energy Reviews, 64*, 237–247. https://doi.org/10.1016/J.RSER.2016.06.008

IEA. (2020). *Renewables 2020.* https://www.iea.org/reports/renewables-2020

IPCC. (2021). *Sixth assessment report, climate change 2021: The physical science basis.* https://www.ipcc.ch/assessment-report/ar6/

Irlam, G. A. (1988). William Armstrong's hydraulic engine and pumps at Cragside. *Industrial Archaeology Review, 11*(1), 68–74. https://doi.org/10.1179/iar.1988.11.1.68

Keller, J., & Kroposki, B. (2010, January). *Understanding fault characteristics of inverter-based distributed energy resources.* (Vol. 48). http://www.osti.gov/bridge

Kroposki, B., Johnson, B., Zhang, Y., Gevorgian, V., Denholm, P., Hodge, B. M., & Hannegan, B. (2017). Achieving a 100% renewable grid: Operating electric power systems with extremely high levels of variable renewable energy. *IEEE Power and Energy Magazine, 15*(2), 61–73. https://doi.org/10.1109/MPE.2016.2637122

Lasseter, R. H., Chen, Z., & Pattabiraman, D. (2020). Grid-forming inverters: A critical asset for the power grid. *IEEE Journal of Emerging and Selected Topics in Power Electronics, 8*(2), 925–935. https://doi.org/10.1109/JESTPE.2019.2959271

Mancarella, P., & Billimoria, F. (2021). The fragile grid: The physics and economics of security services in low-carbon power systems. *IEEE Power and Energy Magazine, 19*(2), 79–88. https://doi.org/10.1109/MPE.2020.3043570

Parag, Y., & Sovacool, B. K. (2016). Electricity market design for the prosumer era. *Nature Energy, 1*(4). https://doi.org/10.1038/nenergy.2016.32

Parkinson, G. (2021). No need for synchronous assets in zero emissions grid, says Tesla. *RenewEconomy.* https://reneweconomy.com.au/no-need-for-synchronous-assets-in-zero-emissions-grid-says-tesla/

Quint, R., Dangelmaier, L., Green, I., Edelson, D., Ganugula, V., Kaneshiro, R., Pigeon, J., Quaintance, B., Riesz, J., & Stringer, N. (2019). Transformation of the grid: The impact of distributed energy resources on bulk power systems. *IEEE Power and Energy Magazine, 17*(6), 35–45. https://doi.org/10.1109/MPE.2019.2933071

Schweppe, F. C. (1978, July). Power systems "2000": Hierarchical control strategies. *IEEE Spectrum.*

Sommerfeld, J., Buys, L., & Vine, D. (2017). Residential consumers' experiences in the adoption and use of solar PV. *Energy Policy, 105*, 10–16. https://doi.org/10.1016/J.ENPOL.2017.02.021

Sousa, T., Soares, T., Pinson, P., Moret, F., Baroche, T., & Sorin, E. (2019). Peer-to-peer and community-based markets: A comprehensive review. *Renewable and Sustainable Energy Reviews, 104*, 367–378. https://doi.org/10.1016/j.rser.2019.01.036

Sulzberger, C. L. (2003). Triumph of ac-from Pearl Street to Niagara. *IEEE Power and Energy Magazine, 1*(3), 64–67.

Weaver, J. (2021). Tesla powerwalls in California join the movement to create virtual power plants. *PV Magazine.* https://www.pv-magazine.com/2021/07/26/tesla-powerwalls-in-california-join-the-movement-to-create-virtual-power-plants/

CHAPTER 3

Evolving Roles in Distribution Networks: Resource Coordination and Control Under the Emergence of the Distribution System Operator

Abstract In this chapter, we focus upon the emergent models of operation and coordination of decentralised energy resources and cover the roles played by distribution utilities and operators, in moving from a passive network operator to an increasingly active scheduler and coordinator of DERs, to a platform provider. We provide a breakdown of elements underpinning the functions of both a network operator and a system operator and highlight the differentiated operational and market considerations in managing a distribution-level market relative to a transmission network. We argue that the traditional modes of operation and coordination that have been successful in the transmission context may not necessarily apply to distributed networks requiring regulators to think more broadly about alternative operating and governance modes for the new DSO.

Keywords Distribution system operator · Peer-to-peer networks · Prosumer market design

© The Author(s), under exclusive license to Springer Nature Switzerland AG 2022
R. Poudineh et al., *Electricity Distribution Networks in the Decentralisation Era*,
https://doi.org/10.1007/978-3-030-98069-6_3

3.1 Introduction

The growth of distributed energy resources marks a transformational shift in the approach to the operation of the electricity network. First in terms of the broad directionality of flows, the electricity system has shifted from a unidirectional network to a bidirectional network. Where electricity used to flow consistently from large generation resources in the high-voltage (HV) transmission network through to consumers in the medium-voltage (MV) and low-voltage (LV) distribution networks, it now flows bidirectionally depending upon patterns of consumption and DER availability. Flows can vary significantly on temporal basis, with net consumption at a distribution network or customer level quickly switching to net injection into the grid. Indeed many regions around the world (such as California and many regions in the National Electricity Market), system demand during the middle of the day is declining at rapid rates as a result of large-scale DER deployment with an oversupply of generation needing to be curtailed in some manner (AEMO, 2020; CAISO, 2021). Indeed in the NEM region of South Australia, minimum demand is projected to go negative within the next two years. Moreover, flows can also be driven by locational dynamics, depending upon local weather patterns and the scale of DER deployment in particular distribution network areas. As a result, the operation of the distribution grid and its interaction with the transmission grid is likely to become increasingly complex.

The implications for operational management of networks at low levels of DER penetration were considered minimal, resulting in a relatively 'light touch' approach to the operation of the distribution network. However, given (i) the pace at which DER penetration has grown, (ii) the development and rollout of DER storage and control technology with more active and dynamic functionality, and (iii) the expansion of business models for DER aggregation and orchestration, there is an urgent need for a reconsideration of system and network operation protocols and the roles, responsibilities, and capabilities of the electricity market agents in the distribution grid. This is resonant in calls for a shift in the operational model from a relatively passive network operation to active distribution system and platform operation. This poses important questions on the role (objectives and functionalities), organisation, governance, and incentives of the new 'distribution system operator'.

In this chapter we begin by describing the core roles and functionalities of the transmission system operator that evolved from the liberalisation of electricity markets and the need to competitively optimise generation scheduling. We then specify core power system requirements and clarify the technical emphasis that is important for distribution networks in a DER heavy grid.

In the following sections, we set out the differentiating factors relevant to a distribution-level DER-rich grid, including the lack of visibility and predictability in systems control and coordination, challenges in obtaining the requisite information to run a direct scheduled system, the need to facilitate P2P markets along with secure distribution operations and the need to coordinate between transmission and distribution operation. Given these factors we argue that this distinguishes the functional responsibilities of a system operator from a network operator and provides the rationale for more active but differentiated operational management of distribution system.

3.2 Operator Roles and Functionalities

The liberalisation of the electricity sector beginning in the 1990s and continuing into the 2000s changed the organisational structures and roles for the operation and scheduling of generation resources to meet load. The unbundling of vertically integrated electric utilities into generation, transmission and distribution, and retail segments required the competitive and transparent operational scheduling of generation to meet load. Two models emerged for the organisation of the system operator. Many regions of the US, Canada, and Australia created new standalone entities known as the Independent System Operators (ISOs) or Regional Transmission Operators (RTOs), in which the role of system operation and management was delegated (Pollitt, 2011). By contrast, other regions such as in the UK[1] or Europe retained the system operation role within existing transmission companies (either state-owned or privatised), often with differing degrees of divisions and separation from network planning operations. This latter model is typically known as the transmission system operator (TSO) model.

---

[1] In the UK, the operations of the Electricity System Operator (ESO) have to date been retained within the transmission network owner and operator National Grid UK. However, the intent is for the system operator role to be removed from the network owner and made independent (Ofgem, 2021).

The role of system operator, emerging originally in a transmission context, has evolved to provide a range of critical services (Stoft, 2002). Core to system operator role in both ISO and TSO models is the functionality that includes the (i) commitment, scheduling, and pricing of generation and load at and ahead of real time and (ii) operational constraints and congestion management (both intra- and inter-regional). In a large-scale centralised transmission system, the principles of optimal power flow (OPF) and economic dispatch has provided an elegant reconciliation between the physical and economics of power supply and has usefully guided the development of this operator functionality (Hogan, 2018). Regions around the world typically run one or more variants of security constrained economic dispatch (SCED) that enables generation and load to be scheduled and dispatched and cleared (priced generally via marginal pricing frameworks). In addition to the scheduling role, other critical roles of the system operator include (iii) the procurement of system services, such as frequency and voltage response, (iv) monitoring of operational reliability and interventions, directions and redispatch of systems to manage security and reliability, (v) the provision of forecast and real-time market and system information, (vi) financial settlement and clearing, and (vii) emergency management and system restart (Pollitt, 2011). Certain operators also incorporate system and network planning, network connection/access and network augmentation roles in extension to day-to-day grid operations.

In addition to the traditional primacy of centralised generation in energy balancing, transmission-level resources also provide a variety of operational services to distribution grids including voltage support and system strength. In concordance with the rollout of more active DER, distribution-level resources are also increasingly providing energy and system services to the central grid (Eid et al., 2016) including most evidently frequency control (AEMO, 2021) and have the potential to provide local services (Meegahapola et al., 2021; Riaz & Mancarella, 2019). Interactions between the delivery of energy and services between transmission and distribution grids require scheduling and operational coordination (Saint-Pierre & Mancarella, 2017) between transmission system operators (TSOs) and distribution system operators (DSOs).

3.3 Power System Requirements

Before specifying the functionalities of a distribution system operator, we must first specify the power system requirements and clarify the emphasis as it relates to distribution systems. Four critical power system requirements underpin the operation of an AC-electrical grid comprising (i) resource adequacy and capability that there resources adequate to ensure a real-time balancing of active power generation and demand (ii) frequency management—the ability to set and maintain system frequency within acceptable limits under normal conditions and under disturbances, (iii) voltage management—the ability to maintain voltages within acceptable limits under normal conditions and under disturbances, and (iv) system restoration—the ability to restore the system in the event of interruption (Billimoria et al., 2020; Conejo & Baringo, 2018; Johnson et al., 2017).

While the core technical attributes required for the reliable and secure operation of an AC-network remain consistent across transmission and distribution grid, the physical and market characteristics pose differential operational risks and require distinct operational emphases. The operation of the system at a distribution level is distinct from transmission at a number of levels, which must be reflected in any operational management framework.

Voltage stability and power flows are of particular focus in distribution grids. Operational challenges for voltage control can emerge where dynamic temporal shifts in line loading within a local area can adversely affect absolute voltage levels (I. M. Dudurych, 2021). Examples include high rooftop solar penetrations in local regions resulting in over-voltages at times of high solar export (Meegahapola & Littler, 2017; Watson et al., 2016) or uncontrolled electric vehicle charging resulting in under-voltages (de Hoog et al., 2014; Sun et al., 2020). Automatic control mechanisms similar to the ones that have underpinned voltage management in large-scale synchronous systems of the transmission grid have to date been unavailable in distribution grids under passive DER control (Meegahapola & Littler, 2017), though voltage response at the transmission level can support locationally adjacent distribution (I. Dudurych et al., 2016). Congestion is a closely related and important challenge for DSOs. The bidirectional and uncertain flow of power in DER-rich grids may result in congestions at certain points in the distribution network.

The implications of congestion include asset overloading, voltage deviations and potential cascading failures. As such, the management and mitigation of distribution system congestion is an important component of DSO functionality. However, as will be discussed in the following sections, the direct adoption of approaches that have worked in the transmission grid may not necessarily work in a distribution network with diverse and dynamic consumption and generation patterns.

Power quality, which commonly takes into account two important aspects: harmonic distortion of the network voltage and transient voltage variations, are also of enhanced relevance in distribution grids especially in areas with a high penetration of DERs (Zubo et al., 2017). On a related point, distribution grids also tend to rely upon central provision of system strength, traditionally by large-sale synchronous resources but increasingly also from advanced inverter technology (Bowman et al., 2019; Lasseter et al., 2020). As against this, while distributed resources can meaningfully contribute to frequency control, frequency as a system-wide parameter tends to be controlled and managed at a centralised grid level (Püschel-Løvengreen et al., 2020). Grids with rapid DER deployment face the further prospect of negative minimum operational demand. Two particular issues are highlighted relate to (i) increased complexity and risks during islanded operation of the region (which while not considered an N-1 contingency—is part of a suite of risks requiring protection (ii) the risk of voltage-driven instability and disconnection of distributed inverters in low system strength conditions. Of the range of measures highlighted to mitigate the issue, of particular criticality is the urgent enhancement of DER controllability and response (both as part of normal operation, as well as response under disturbance) and real-time management of controlled load curtailment (Billimoria, 2021).

3.4 Visibility, Predictability, and Controllability of DER-Rich Grids

In a transmission context, the approach to market and system scheduling is underpinned by the principles of security constrained economic dispatch (SCED) (Hogan, 2014). At a high level, under a SCED approach, the system operator takes in bids and offers for energy and ancillary services, and optimally schedules resources subject to security constraints. Locational marginal prices (LMP) are then produced as an outturn of the dispatch optimisation that prices electricity based on its scarcity on a locational and temporal basis (though noting that zonal or regional pricing rather than LMP dominates in many regions and remains an open area of discussion) (Simshauser et al., 2021). This process takes place in real time, as well as in one of many short-term ahead markets (including day-ahead and intraday). The implementation of this model, in liberalised electricity markets around the world, varies from direct implementations of SCED—such in regions as PJM or the NEM which optimises dispatch and prices electricity subject to many thousands of technical, system, resource, and stability constraints—to more indirect approaches which begin with an economic merit-order and redispatches the system based on technical requirements (as is the case with regions such as the UK) (Hogan, 2014; National Grid, 2021). Two points are important here. First, regardless of the particular implementation the formulation of system constraints are dependent upon the provision of highly granular resource information set that spans availability, technical limits, and control systems of the generator or resource (Tam, 2011). This assists the operator in being able to develop constraints that are reflective of system physics and that will provide a secure operating envelope for the system. Knowledge of such technical and control system parameters is typically submitted to the operator as part of the network connection and access process. Operators will run detailed analyses—often including granular dynamic simulation to then develop static constraints that can be incorporated into a dispatch optimisation (which is typically linear or mixed-integer linear in formulation—this is important for solution scalability outlined later) (AEMO, 2020). Second, conformance with dispatch is generally binding upon generators as part of connection agreements and accession to system rules and procedures, though the nature of obligations for conformance can vary based on resource type and size. This gives operators confidence in the bindingness of dispatch as the lynchpin for secure operations.

The deployment of DER poses a number of challenges for the applicability of a SCED in a distribution network. Concerns have been raised with respect to the visibility, predictability, and controllability of a DER-rich network. DSOs and energy markets need to have some visibility on a large number of small power injections (Tarazona et al., 2009). The concept of the virtual power plant (or VPP) was developed to enhance the visibility and control of DER to system operators and other market participants (Pudjianto et al., 2007). However, while aggregation may be appropriate for scheduling transmission-level services provided by distributed resources (Quint et al., 2019), direct scheduling of energy at the local level requires clear visibility of parameters including availability, generation, and voltages (O'Connell et al., 2018). While monitoring technology and applications can improve such visibility, it needs to be deployed at scale and at a highly granular level to be able to incorporate direct scheduling, which may be difficult in a consumer setting introducing challenges with respect to the consumer's willingness to provide such information. Increased interconnection and integration will also introduce cyber-vulnerabilities into the grid, which needs to be managed in a privacy preserving manner. Further, access to information on how and when a DER will respond including details on automation, control, and protection systems may be even harder to come by, given its commercial IP value. Both of which are important for developing appropriate line-level constraints.

Challenges are also raised with respect to controllability. (Charbonnier, 2021) provides a review of research trends and a taxonomy of paradigms for distributed energy resource coordination as between direct control, and indirect control (which includes mediated coordination, bilateral coordination, and implicit coordination models). It is suggested that while direct control may be applicable to select cases, or where DER is providing wholesale services, indirect control supported by automation and operating envelopes may have more applicability in a consumer-centric environment. Consumers may have limited willingness to be directly engaged and controlled with respect to their energy use, and to agree to follow central dispatch instructions. While it may be workable for a small subset of consumers or consumers in specific settings (e.g., micro-grids), as a whole, consumers may be unwilling to accede to that level of control. Despite advances in optimisation technologies, there are also software challenges in the scale of dispatch control required, which for many systems is likely to be computationally intractable. Distributed optimisation techniques are likely to be more appropriate for such applications (Caramanis et al., 2016; R. D. Tabors et al., 2016) but potential convergence challenges imply that rather than fixed schedules, the concept of an 'operating envelope', where resources agree to be bounded within a range of generation and consumption values, may be more appropriate for such an application.

The impact of pricing is a relevant consideration in a DER framework. As outlined above the concept of LMP is critical to optimising the system and managing market incentives. The price is intended to provide suitable financial incentive to generators and load to dispatch at optimal levels and not to deviate from the schedule, which in a wholesale and primarily commercial context has proved effective (Simshauser, 2018). The concept of a Distributed Locational Marginal Pricing (DLMP) has been introduced as a pricing principle, extending the well-known LMP to distribution grid level context (R. Tabors et al., 2017; R. D. Tabors et al., 2016). However, at a distribution level, there are multiple reasons as to why prosumers may consume or generate energy including reasons which are unlinked to commercial incentives such as environmental or social incentives (Morstyn & McCulloch, 2019; Tushar et al., 2019), suggesting that centralisation of dispatch and dispatch conformance may be challenging. As an alternative, in (Morstyn et al., 2020), DLMPs are used to provide high-level incentives to consumers, but an operator must manage risk associated with revenue imbalances.

The nature of TSO–DSO coordination implies order-of-magnitude shifts in the need for scalability of dispatch algorithms to clear transmission and distribution-level markets. Solution techniques need to ensure that TSOs and/or DSOs will be able to solve validation and dispatch problems on ultra large networks. Most TSOs continue rely upon linear or mixed-integer security constrained commitment and dispatch approximations, whereas distribution networks have used single-phase AC optimal power flow (OPF) to capture technical constraints and non-linearities of distribution networks of medium-scale DER connected to MV levels (Givisiez et al., 2020). The interaction between transmission and distribution highlights the need for comprehensive three-phase approaches that can handle unbalanced networks and multiple voltages levels, with distributed or iterative approaches as a potential avenue towards system optimisation (Caramanis et al., 2016; R. Tabors et al., 2017; R. D. Tabors et al., 2016). Under the first DSO operating model mentioned in the next section, the computational requirements are likely to be largest as the TSO takes primacy in scheduling all resources across the entire network—transmission and distribution. This implies transmission as well as distribution-level schedules, constraints, and prices. The second and third models, where the DSO takes a greater role in managing operational security and local network constraints, are likely to mute the computational requirements and allow for improved tractability, as optimisations and coordination frameworks are applied over smaller local distribution regions. Furthermore, given the feedback linkages between the TSO and DSO are inherent in these models, they also open the possibility for iterative or distributed approaches to computing dispatch solutions.

3.5 Operating in a P2P Context

The growth of DER has also fuelled the emergence of peer-to-peer (P2P) markets for electricity trading. Leveraging upon P2P sharing and consumer-centric business models, the concept of P2P market has been developed in electricity to enable prosumers to trade with each other, either by selling their excess energy or by reducing the demand of energy (Tushar et al., 2020). Under the theoretical framework of P2P markets, prosumers are in control of setting the terms of transactions and the delivering of goods and services, with little or no influence from a central controller. However, this is challenging currently in an electricity network given the need to manage operational security (Park & Yong, 2017).

As such this puts the DSO in a slightly invidious position with the responsibility for operational security in a region where the political economy is supportive of such facilitation (Guerrero et al., 2018). Ultimately, however, such frameworks must yield to the primacy of physics and the prioritisation of operational security. Operational frameworks may also need to manage the growth of P2P trading between consumers on flexibility (Morstyn et al., 2019) and uncertainty (Zhang et al., 2020) on an intra- and inter-distribution grid levels. Yet such trading must also respect operational voltage and network constraints (Guerrero et al., 2018; Morstyn et al., 2020). Properly coordinated, Morstyn et al. (2018) argue that regional aggregation and peer-to-peer (P2P) could also incentivise the formation of federated power plants that deliver central and inter-grid services.[2] Distribution system operation would thus have a dual functionality of neutral market facilitation as a platform for P2P trading (Vanhove, 2020), which may work separately to facilitating and coordinating orchestrated DER service provision to a wholesale market. Such functionality may be delegated to separate parties, or may be managed by one operator, but coordination between the roles must be facilitated.

---

[2] There are also additional complications relating to the operation of DC grids, both independently and in relation to the interaction between AC and DC grids—which may have relevance to distribution-level microgrids. An analysis of the granular technical requirements is out of the scope of this chapter, and interested readers are instead referred to (Nejabatkhah et al., 2019). We do note however that these are additional complications that an operator of DER-rich grid may have to contend with and manage.

3.6 DSO Operating Models

The operation of a distribution centric market involves a multitude of system functionalities including:

- Grid operator—responsibility for real-time operation of resources within the distribution grid
- Distributed energy resource manager (DERM)—responsible for coordinating and optimising DERs owned and/or operated by a multitude of parties (individuals, aggregators, utilities, retailers).
- Market operator—management of a platform for bids and offers for distribution-level energy and services
- Operational and Investment Planner—Short, medium, and long-term system and investment planning.

The operating model for a DSO involves the allocation of such roles in a manner that is optimal for the distribution grid, but also reflective of the interactions and coordination with the central wholesale/transmission-level grid.

To this end, a range of DSO coordination models are emergent in the literature. Givisiez et al. (2020) provide a taxonomy involving three generalised classifications.

In the first model, termed a TSO-centric model, is a highly centralised model in which the TSO, operating under either an independent system operator (ISO) or as a utility operator, subsumes responsibility for many of the key functionalities of a DSO. The TSO performs core system and market operator roles including the economic dispatch of transmission energy resources (conventional bulk generation) and DER considering network constraints for both the distribution and transmission networks (Givisiez et al., 2020). Central to this model is the primacy of one central scheduler making decisions across both networks. The DSO's primary responsibility from a scheduling perspective is to provide distribution network real-time operational data to the TSO to incorporate into constraint framework. Implicit in this model is direct control and scheduling of DER together with dispatch conformance requirements, akin to resources operating at a wholesale level. Black & Veatch (2020) explicates two sub-models which are differentiated by the allocation of the DERM role, allocated to the TSO in a TSO-only model and to the distribution utility in a TSO-Hybrid Utility model.

A centralised model may be considered intuitive, and as a ready extension of the existing TSO model. Moreover by allocating most roles to a single entity the challenge of coordination may be simplified. Further, the TSO is also free from conflicts with DER asset ownership and distribution network management roles. Against this are significant challenges associated with the scale of coordination and computational effort required. Moreover given the challenges associated with direct control of distribution resources, the wholesale transmission dispatch model may not necessarily directly suit the distribution network. The distribution network also involves different operational challenges relative to a transmission network that an ISO may be less experienced in managing.

In the second model, referred to as the TSO–DSO hybrid model, the roles relating to the economic dispatch of transmission and distribution resources, bid validation and formulation of local distribution-level constraints are split between the TSO and a DSO entity (either the existing distribution utility or a new entity) (Gerard et al., 2018). Black & Veatch (2020) suggest that a DLMP type pricing framework is likely to be adopted in such frameworks. Often the DSO is allocated roles relating to bid validation and distribution-level constraint management with a close coordination with the TSO to transfer bidding, availability, and dispatch information (Givisiez et al., 2020). In essence the DSO is responsible for managing the distribution-level security envelope and will only validate bids that are in conformity with that envelope. This also enables the DSO to utilise and procure DER services for the purposes of managing distribution-level operational security. This model provides the flexibility for both direct and as well as indirect control of resources. The advantage of this classification of models is that it adopts a more nuanced allocation of roles to parties more likely to be better placed to manage it. For example, the entity most familiar with the operation and management of distribution-level constraints would retain such functionalities, while wholesale market coordination would remain at the ISO level. Computational tractability could also be enhanced through distributed approaches to scheduling and pricing, and operational data transfer requirements are limited (Givisiez et al., 2020). However under this approach the coordination processes are more complex and require specific management focus. Moreover, policymakers must be aware of the potential conflicts associated with the role of system operation and ownership of assets. This however could be mitigated through the establishment of a new independent DSO entity.

Finally the third model, referred to as the DSO-centric model, the DSO is responsible for validating, coordinating, and aggregating all DER services (Le Cadre et al., 2019). The DSO essentially becomes the aggregator of energy and services on a regional level as well as managing operational security and the coordination of local services. This model provides the DSO with greatest autonomy in scheduling resources either under a direct or indirect approach. Under this approach the DSO takes on the role of platform provider for the enablement of peer-to-peer trading, either as a commercial utility or as an independent entity (Black & Veatch, 2020). However, given the potential for operational security challenges associated with this, a last-resort provider role may also be required under such a model. The advantage of such a role is the potential for rapid and expanded facilitation of DER and P2P trading, as well as housing the operational role in an entity familiar with distribution grid operation. Computational requirements are also made more tractable under a P2P framework, with the possibility of distributed coordination and execution of contracts. However, as against this, large-scale implementation of this model may introduce significant challenges for operational security (managing voltages, system strength, etc.) requiring resource redispatch and trade revocation (where security is at risk). The system may also require significant backup and grid support services (for voltage and stability support) and significant investment in the network to enable unconstrained or less constrained flows.

3.7 Conclusions and Policy Implications

Electricity distribution networks find themselves in a new operating environment where the directionality of flows in the electricity grid is subject to disruption. The emerging role of local resources in providing system-wide as well as local services suggests that operational frameworks can no longer be fully segregated across voltage boundaries. Correspondingly, transmission-level resources are also likely to play an increasingly important function supporting and facilitating the delivery of DER energy and services, through providing voltage support or system strength. As such, transmission and distribution networks are likely to become increasingly interlinked and inter-dependent.

Traditional operational models for electricity systems focus upon a central operator with responsibility for direct scheduling in the market and providing efficient and incentive compatible prices to participants. A precondition of this model is the availability of accurate and timely information on the state of the grid, and an explicit agreement between the operator and participants to follow the rules of central dispatch.

Each of the three classifications of DER operational models have advantages and disadvantages, and there is unlikely to be a best or one size fits all model that suits all electricity grids. However given the challenges associated with the visibility, predictability, and controllability of DERs suggest that careful consideration is required when deciding upon operating models. The assumption that the style of operation that has worked in the transmission grid context can be simply transferred to a consumer-centric environment is unlikely to be successful. Peer-to-peer markets add an additional wrinkle where the ultimate objective of such markets is to remove, as much as possible, the presence of the trusted intermediary, as against the need to maintain operational security in a complex electricity network.

As such, it is incumbent upon to review and investigate alternative models of system operation away from the traditional top-down centralised hierarchy. This should include consideration of indirect and implicit models of coordination that leverage upon the automation of control subject to incentives. In such areas, multi-agent facilitation models that harness the rapidity and automation potential of key DER function at minimal impact to service quality and amenity may provide an interesting complement to direct scheduling of specific resources. New governance models and segregation of roles may also be considered including the consideration of models that incorporate performance management, incentivises, and penalties on the operator or platform providers themselves. This may work to ensure best-in-class participation in this essential component of the electricity markets function.

REFERENCES

AEMO. (2020). *Integrated system plan.* https://aemo.com.au/en/energy-systems/major-publications/integrated-system-plan-isp/2020-integrated-system-plan-isp

AEMO. (2021). *Virtual power plant demonstrations knowledge sharing report 3.* https://arena.gov.au/assets/2021/02/aemo-virtual-power-plant-demonstrations-report-3.pdf

Billimoria, F. (2021). Over the edge—Energy risk trading in a negative demand environment. *Energy Forum, Second Quarter*, (2). https://www.iaee.org/en/publications/newsletterdl.aspx?id=954

Billimoria, F., Mancarella, P., & Poudineh, R. (2020). *Market design for system security in low-carbon electricity grids: From the physics to the economics* (Issue June). https://doi.org/10.26889/9781784671600

Black & Veatch. (2020). *Distribution System Operator (DSO) Models for utility stakeholders*. https://www.bv.com/sites/default/files/2020-02/20Distribution%20System%20Operator%20Models%20for%20Utility%20Stakeholders%20WEB%20updated%20022720.pdf

Bowman, D., Ramasubramanian, D., McCann, R., Farantatos, E., Gaikwad, A., & Caspary, J. (2019). SPP grid strength study with high inverter-based resource penetration. *51st North American Power Symposium, NAPS 2019*. https://doi.org/10.1109/NAPS46351.2019.9000309

CAISO. (2021). *Behind-the-meter solar impact to demand and operations*. https://www.wecc.org/Administrative/Motley-Behind-the-Meter%20Solar%20Impact%20to%20Demand%20Forecasting_February%202021.pdf

Caramanis, M., Ntakou, E., Hogan, W. W., Chakrabortty, A., & Schoene, J. (2016). Co-optimization of power and reserves in dynamic T&D power markets with nondispatchable renewable generation and distributed energy resources. *Proceedings of the IEEE, 104*(4), 807–836. https://doi.org/10.1109/JPROC.2016.2520758

Charbonnier, F. (2021). *Coordination of resources at the edge of the electricity grid: Systematic review and classification*.

Conejo, A. J., & Baringo, L. (2018). Power system operations. *Springer International Publishing*. https://doi.org/10.1007/978-3-319-69407-8

de Hoog, J., Alpcan, T., Member, S., Brazil, M., Anne Thomas, D., & Mareels, I. (2014). *Optimal Charging of Electric Vehicles Taking Distribution Network Constraints into Account*. https://doi.org/10.1109/TPWRS.2014.2318293

Dudurych, I., Burke, M., Fisher, L., Eager, M., & Kelly, K. (2016, August). Operational security challenges and tools for a synchronous power system with high penetration of non-conventional sources. *CIGRE Session, 46*, 1–11.

Dudurych, I. M. (2021). The impact of renewables on operational security: Operating power systems that have extremely high penetrations of nonsynchronous renewable sources. *IEEE Power and Energy Magazine, 19*(2), 37–45. https://doi.org/10.1109/MPE.2020.3043614

Eid, C., Codani, P., Perez, Y., Reneses, J., & Hakvoort, R. (2016). Managing electric flexibility from distributed energy resources: A review of incentives for market design. *Renewable and Sustainable Energy Reviews, 64*, 237–247. https://doi.org/10.1016/J.RSER.2016.06.008

Gerard, H., Rivero, E. I., & Six, D. (2018). Coordination between transmission and distribution system operators in the electricity sector: A conceptual framework. *Utilities Policy, 50*, 40–48. https://doi.org/10.1016/J.JUP.2017.09.011

Givisiez, A. G., Petrou, K., & Ochoa, L. F. (2020). A review on TSO-DSO coordination models and solution techniques. *Electric Power Systems Research, 189*, 106659. https://doi.org/10.1016/J.EPSR.2020.106659

Guerrero, J., Chapman, A. C., & Verbic, G. (2018). Decentralized P2P energy trading under network constraints in a low-voltage network. *IEEE Transactions on Smart Grid, 1–10.* https://doi.org/10.1109/TSG.2018.2878445

Hogan, W. W. (2014). Electricity market design and efficient pricing: Applications for New England and beyond. *Electricity Journal, 27*(7), 23–49. https://doi.org/10.1016/j.tej.2014.07.009

Hogan, W. W. (2018, October 4). *Can electricity markets meet the challenge of meeting non-market objectives?*. https://sites.hks.harvard.edu/fs/whogan/Hogan_HEPG_100418r.pdf

Johnson, B., Denholm, P., Kroposki, B., & Hodge, B. (2017, April). Achieving a 100% renewable grid. *IEEE Power and Energy Magazine, 61–73,.* https://doi.org/10.1109/MPE.2016.2637122

Lasseter, R. H., Chen, Z., & Pattabiraman, D. (2020). Grid-forming inverters: A critical asset for the power grid. *IEEE Journal of Emerging and Selected Topics in Power Electronics, 8*(2), 925–935. https://doi.org/10.1109/JESTPE.2019.2959271

Le Cadre, H., Mezghani, I., & Papavasiliou, A. (2019). A game-theoretic analysis of transmission-distribution system operator coordination. *European Journal of Operational Research, 274*(1), 317–339. https://doi.org/10.1016/J.EJOR.2018.09.043

Meegahapola, L., & Littler, T. (2017). Distributed solar-PV generation: Impact on voltage control and stability. In *Handbook of Distributed Generation: Electric Power Technologies, Economics and Environmental Impacts* (pp. 317–342). Springer International Publishing. https://doi.org/10.1007/978-3-319-51343-0_10

Meegahapola, L., Mancarella, P., Flynn, D., & Moreno, R. (2021). Power system stability in the transition to a low carbon grid: A techno-economic perspective on challenges and opportunities. *WIREs Energy and Environment*, e399. https://doi.org/10.1002/wene.399

Morstyn, T., Farrell, N., Darby, S. J., & McCulloch, M. D. (2018). Using peer-to-peer energy-trading platforms to incentivize prosumers to form federated power plants. *Nature Energy, 3*(2), 94–101. https://doi.org/10.1038/s41560-017-0075-y

Morstyn, T., & McCulloch, M. D. (2019). Multiclass energy management for peer-to-peer energy trading driven by prosumer preferences. *IEEE Transactions on Power Systems, 34*(5), 4005–4014. https://doi.org/10.1109/TPWRS.2018.2834472

Morstyn, T., Teytelboym, A., Hepburn, C., & McCulloch, M. D. (2020). Integrating P2P energy trading with probabilistic distribution locational marginal pricing. *IEEE Transactions on Smart Grid, 11*(4), 3095–3106. https://doi.org/10.1109/TSG.2019.2963238

Morstyn, T., Teytelboym, A., & McCulloch, M. D. (2019). Bilateral contract networks for peer-to-peer energy trading. *IEEE Transactions on Smart Grid, 10*(2), 2026–2035. https://doi.org/10.1109/TSG.2017.2786668

National Grid. (2021). Operability strategy report. *Report.* https://www.nationalgrideso.com/research-publications/system-operability-framework-sof

Nejabatkhah, F., Li, Y. W., & Tian, H. (2019). Power quality control of smart hybrid AC/DC microgrids: An overview. *IEEE Access, 7*, 52295–52318. https://doi.org/10.1109/ACCESS.2019.2912376

O'Connell, A., Taylor, J., Smith, J., & Rogers, L. (2018). Distributed energy resources takes center stage: A renewed spotlight on the distribution planning process. *IEEE Power and Energy Magazine, 16*(6), 42–51. https://doi.org/10.1109/MPE.2018.2862439

Ofgem. (2021). *Review of GB system operation.* https://www.ofgem.gov.uk/publications/review-gb-energy-system-operation

Park, C., & Yong, T. (2017). Comparative review and discussion on P2P electricity trading. *Energy Procedia, 128*, 3–9. https://doi.org/10.1016/j.egypro.2017.09.003

Pollitt, M. J. (2011). *Lessons from the History of Independent System Operators in the Energy Sector, with applications to the Water Sector.* https://www.Researchgate.net/publication/254396599_Lessons_from_the_History_of_Independent_System_Operators_in_the_Energy_Sector_with_applications_to_the_Water_Sector

Pudjianto, D., Ramsay, C., & Strbac, G. (2007). Virtual power plant and system integration of distributed energy resources. *IET Renewable Power Generation, 1*(1), 10–16. https://doi.org/10.1049/IET-RPG:20060023

Püschel-Løvengreen, S., Ghazavi, M., Low, S., & Mancarella, P. (2020). Separation event-constrained optimal power flow to enhance resilience in low-inertia power systems. *Electric Power Systems Research, 189*, 106678. https://doi.org/10.1016/j.epsr.2020.106678

Quint, R., Dangelmaier, L., Green, I., Edelson, D., Ganugula, V., Kaneshiro, R., Pigeon, J., Quaintance, B., Riesz, J., & Stringer, N. (2019). Transformation of the grid: The impact of distributed energy resources on bulk power systems. *IEEE Power and Energy Magazine, 17*(6), 35–45. https://doi.org/10.1109/MPE.2019.2933071

Riaz, S., & Mancarella, P. (2019). On feasibility and flexibility operating regions of virtual power plants and TSO/DSO interfaces. *2019 IEEE Milan PowerTech, PowerTech, 2019*, 1–6. https://doi.org/10.1109/PTC.2019.8810638

Saint-Pierre, A., & Mancarella, P. (2017). Active distribution system management: A dual-horizon scheduling framework for DSO/TSO interface under uncertainty. *IEEE Transactions on Smart Grid, 8*(5), 2186–2197. https://doi.org/10.1109/TSG.2016.2518084

Simshauser, P. (2018). On intermittent renewable generation & the stability of Australia's national electricity market. *Energy Economics, 72*(May), 1–19. https://doi.org/10.1016/j.eneco.2018.02.006

Simshauser, P., Billimoria, F., & Rogers, C. (2021). *Optimising VRE plant capacity in renewable energy zones* (No. 2121). www.eprg.group.cam.ac.uk

Stoft, S. (2002). *Power system economics: Designing markets for electricity* (1st ed.). Wiley-IEEE Press. https://ieeexplore.ieee.org/xpl/bkabstractplus.jsp?bkn=5264048

Sun, W., Neumann, F., & Harrison, G. P. (2020). Robust scheduling of electric vehicle charging in LV distribution networks under uncertainty. *IEEE Transactions on Industry Applications, 56*(5), 5785–5795. https://doi.org/10.1109/TIA.2020.2983906

Tabors, R., Caramanis, M., Ntakou, E., Parker, G., Van Alstyne, M., Centolella, P., & Hornby, R. (2017). Distributed energy resources: New markets and new products. *Proceedings of the 50th Hawaii International Conference on System Sciences (2017), 1*, 2993–3002. https://doi.org/10.24251/hicss.2017.362

Tabors, R. D., Ph, D., Caramanis, T., & Tcr, R. (2016). *Valuing Distributed Energy Resources (DER) via Distribution Locational Marginal Prices (DLMP) LMP from Transmission to the Meter* ... (pp. 1–13).

Tam, S. (2011). Real-time security-constrained economic dispatch and commitment in the PJM : Experiences and challenges. *FERC software conference*. https://cms.ferc.gov/sites/default/files/2020-05/20110629082452-Jun29-SesC1-Tam-PJM_0.pdf

Tarazona, C., Muscholl, M., Lopez, R., & Passelergue, J. C. (2009). Integration of distributed energy resources in the operation of energy management systems. *1st IEEE-PES/IAS conference on Sustainable Alternative Energy, SAE 2009—Proceedings*. https://doi.org/10.1109/SAE.2009.5534858

Tushar, W., Saha, T. K., Yuen, C., Morstyn, T., McCulloch, M. D., Poor, H. V., & Wood, K. L. (2019). A motivational game-theoretic approach for peer-to-peer energy trading in the smart grid. *Applied Energy, 243*, 10–20. https://doi.org/10.1016/j.apenergy.2019.03.111

Tushar, W., Saha, T. K., Yuen, C., Smith, D., & Poor, H. V. (2020). Peer-to-peer trading in electricity networks: An overview. *IEEE Transactions on Smart Grid, 11*(4), 3185–3200. https://doi.org/10.1109/TSG.2020.2969657

Vanhove, S. (2020, September). Peer-to-peer electricity trading: Challenges for the distribution system operator (DSO) under EU law. *International conference on the European Energy Market, EEM*. https://doi.org/10.1109/EEM 49802.2020.9221885

Watson, J. D., Watson, N. R., Santos-Martin, D., Wood, A. R., Lemon, S., & Miller, A. J. V. (2016). Impact of solar photovoltaics on the low-voltage distribution network in New Zealand. *IET Generation, Transmission and Distribution, 10*(1), 1–9. https://doi.org/10.1049/iet-gtd.2014.1076

Zhang, Z., Li, R., & Li, F. (2020). A novel peer-to-peer local electricity market for joint trading of energy and uncertainty. *IEEE Transactions on Smart Grid, 11*(2), 1205–1215. https://doi.org/10.1109/TSG.2019.2933574

Zubo, R. H. A., Mokryani, G., Rajamani, H. S., Aghaei, J., Niknam, T., & Pillai, P. (2017). Operation and planning of distribution networks with integration of renewable distributed generators considering uncertainties: A review. *Renewable and Sustainable Energy Reviews, 72*, 1177–1198. https://doi.org/10.1016/J.RSER.2016.10.036

CHAPTER 4

Regulated Charges for Access to and Utilisation of Networks

Abstract The chapter discusses regulated charges as means to finance the infrastructure and coordinate network users. It covers the traditional distinction of one-off charges for connection, which can be deep or shallow, and continuous use-of-system charges, as flat rates, two-part charges for load and energy with different degrees of time and locational differentiation. The chapter spans issues of cost incidence, on feed-in versus withdrawal as well as energy netting and usage approximation. The theoretical overview is illustrated and loosened up by references to international practice. Criteria used to qualify and compare different tariff schemes include suitability for cost recovery and coordination, for efficient allocation and development of network capacity, transaction cost and requirements for information and regulatory oversight and adaptability facing system transitions.

Keywords Network access regime · Network tariff · Use-of-system charges · Two-part tariff

4.1 Introduction

Network users rely on electricity grids to receive and transport the electricity that they consume, generate, and store. To compensate for access to and utilisation of the grid, users pay what is known as 'network charges'. In principle, like any other price, network charges arrange the allocation of a limited resource which is the network capacity in our case.

As networks are natural monopolies, network capacity is supplied from a dominant position. Thus, to enable access to electricity, which is considered an essential service, network charges are mostly regulated to protect consumers, ensure widespread access to electricity, and encourage efficient provision of capacity. As will be discussed in more detail in Chapter 9, monopoly regulation for networks can focus on different aspects of network operation, such as revenue, cost, and prices—or combinations thereof. The regulator can determine a regulated revenue and may leave it up to the network operator to earn it. Alternatively, regulators may approve network cost which network operators are allowed to recover as they see fit. In addition, regulation may also directly target prices. Regulators may either prescribe tariffs or at least set the charging methodology that network operators ought to follow. In practice, regulators often employ a mix of several regulatory approaches to achieve their objectives of ensuring access to reliable and affordable electricity for all users.

In electricity systems where network operation is unbundled from the rest of electricity supply, network charges are set and regulated separately. This is currently the case for example in the European Union, where in most member states network charges account for between a quarter and a third of end users' electricity bill (Eurostat, 2020). In many other countries, for example several parts of the US and GCC countries, network business remains integrated with generation and retail, especially at the distribution level. In such a structure, electricity or utility tariffs include the costs of all elements across supply chain (including the network cost) and thus regulation is concerned with overall energy charges rather than just network tariffs.

A central purpose of network charges is to recover network cost. Building transformers and new lines mean significant investment. This applies particularly to underground assets which are common in distribution grids. These costs of network assets are largely fixed—i.e., they do not vary with utilisation, especially in the short term. Metering and monitoring are other additions to these fixed costs in the sense that they can hardly be decreased by reducing network use. There are however variable costs too. Utilising the network to transport and distribute electricity incurs electricity losses and influences the need for maintenance. Compared to fixed cost of the network, these variable costs are typically significantly lower. This means that fixed costs dominate the cost structure of network utilities. As a result, much like hotel rooms and seats in a cinema or airplane, once the capacity has been made available, utilising it fully hardly increases overall cost of the provider.

With energy systems in transition, electricity networks, particularly at the distribution level, are required to facilitate efficient decentralisation and decarbonisation. This challenge extends beyond the traditional task of supplying inflexible electricity demands for services such as lighting and running appliances. As decarbonisation of the economy based on electrification progresses, the share of flexible demand in consumer load is likely to increase. This is mainly related to utilisation of electricity for transport and heating/cooling services. Increasingly, these flexible electricity demands need to be accommodated. This is on top of the challenge of integration of low-carbon distributed generation.

Network charges are at the core of incentivising new forms of network use and financing required network investments. Evidently, network tariffs can encourage distributed generators to locate in less congested areas or can incentivise consumers to avoid peak hours. Conversely, network tariffs that have historically not been designed for these new user types may provide perverse incentives and lead them to increased strain on the network rather than engage them to relieve it. Currently, we see first accounts of how traditional network tariffs are not fully equipped for future electricity distribution systems. In many countries, new demands are initially poorly coordinated with the grid. This has manifested for example in excessive self-supply with rooftop solar PV installations (EII, 2013; cf. Simshauser, 2016) or electric vehicle charging that overloads the existing grid (cf. Richardson, 2013).

In addition to the economic objectives of efficiently utilising and developing the network infrastructure, regulated charges are often required to reconcile other potentially conflicting social and political goals, such as fairness, simplicity, predictability or transparency (see for example Bonbright, 1961; CEER, 2020). For a diverse body of network users with a high propensity to adapt their network use in order to save network charges, efficient tariffs are typically highly differentiated. This is because differentiated tariffs reflect the individual effect of using the network in a specific way, at a specific location and time and thus enable each network user to optimise their network use accordingly. However, differentiated tariffs typically conflict with requirements of fairness and simplicity. Especially, for private consumers, it is frequently argued that reacting to ever changing network tariffs is too complicated and tedious—i.e., it bears too large transaction costs. Additionally, differentiated charges may be perceived as unfair. Specifically, consumers may not accept that comparable users would be charged differently at various locations or times (Neuteleers et al., 2017).

To inform an opinion on how to strike a balance concerning these different targets for network tariffs while meeting the challenges related to the energy transition, in what follows, this chapter

– provides an overview of different types of tariff schemes,
– discusses their virtues and problems, and
– relates them to the challenges for distribution networks in decarbonisation era.

4.2 Tariff Schemes

Network charges are a combination of one-off, ex-ante payments when connecting to the grid and a recurring ex-post charges for the use of system throughout a certain period. The former reimburses the network operator for enabling access to the grid, whereas the latter recoups the cost of the actual utilisation of access.

Connection charges can be shallow or deep. Shallow connection charges only recover the immediate cost of linking a new user to the existing grid. For a new building, for example, shallow connection involves merely a cable linking the porch with the nearest grid strand. Deep charges, on the other hand, additionally accounts for necessary reinforcements 'deeper' within the existing grid. This extends, for example, to a transformer upgrade required when several users in the same street connect charging equipment for electric vehicles. In theory, deep charges reflect the cost more accurately and thus potentially steer users away from behaviours that cause expensive capacity requirements. Users balance the gain they obtain from a certain capacity requirement with the cost they face. Ideally, thus, the cost users face corresponds to the cost they cause.

Such cost-reflective charges efficiently allocate existing and future network capacity.

To understand this better assume, for example, that an expensive transformer upgrade is required, to increase the connection capacity of households switching to electric heating. If users that connect heat pumps incur high grid charges, some of them may opt for district heating instead. In effect, expensive grid expansion is prevented. Some users, on the other hand, may be willing to accept higher charges, for instance, in areas where district heating is not available. For these users, the additional cost is justified by the benefit they obtain from electric heating. The grid expansion for this type of network use is not prevented by cost-reflective charges. Instead, if users' gain justifies the additional network cost, expanding the grid to connect the heat pumps increases overall welfare and is therefore efficient.

The effort and potential expansion of existing network assets required to connect new users are individual to every connection. Therefore, in practice, it can be difficult to assess deep connection costs and even harder to link them to a specific connection or network use. This is why despite their limited efficiency, shallow connection charges are rather common. With shallow connection charges, part of the connection costs—i.e., the deep or individual part of the connection expenditures—needs to be recovered via so-called use-of-system charges. Furthermore, in order to do justice to requirements concerning predictability and simplicity, network operators may standardise connection charges in menus of listed prices.

Use-of-system charges complement initial connection charges and recurringly collect revenue for the network operator. Unless the network is partially publicly funded, use-of-system charges need to cover all residual costs that are not recovered by connection charges. This includes any remaining deep connection cost, as well as recurring maintenance and operation costs, and the cost of system losses as well as administration and customer service. In some countries, cost of balancing and metering are also included in the network charges whereas in other places it is recovered separately by the network operator or some third responsible party. For the network operator, it can be quite challenging to assign different types of costs incurred, firstly between connection and use-of-system charges and, secondly between the different possible tariff components for the later.

Table 4.1 Overview of components of network tariffs

Tariff components	Fixed	Flat
	per capacity	connected/fuse capacity individual user peak load user peak load coincident with network peak
	per energy volume	actual withdrawal/injection net energy exchange with the grid

Source Authors

Traditionally, use-of-system charges correspond to grid use during a certain period of time—e.g., one year or one month, and are usually presented in some forms of three-part tariffs. This means they can consist of a fixed (i.e., flat) component as well as components based on capacity and electricity volume (see Table 4.1). The weights between these components may vary according to political goals or the characteristics of the distribution system where they apply, such as topology or the type of use. In extreme forms, use-of-system charges could be entirely flat per billing period or purely based on capacity or energy.

In a distribution system where network uses and users' preferences vary, a flat tariff does not reflect cost adequately and therefore fails to efficiently allocate capacity. Nonetheless, a flat tariff is simple, transparent, and predictable. It is thus easy to administer because it has low transaction cost, for both network operator and users and may be perceived as fair.

A capacity component can be based on different aspects of capacity—i.e., connected capacity, individual peak, or coincident peak load (i.e., consumer's load during the period in which electricity network experiences peak demand).

If it is based on connected capacity, the tariff is essentially flat unless users alter their fuse size. An increase of fuse capacity could, for example, become necessary if the user wishes to charge an electric vehicle. Conversely, a reduction of fuse capacity might make sense when a building is repurposed from industrial to commercial or refurbished for higher energy efficiency.

Network operators can also base capacity charges on a user's maximum utilised capacity—i.e., individual peak load. This is measured, resp.

approximated, or can usually be predicted with little effort. With individual load as charging base, network users are in control of their network bill. Particularly, commercial and industrial network users have adapted operating schedules to increase utilisation of their connection and minimise individual network load. Yet, charges based on individual peak usage potentially incentivise users to reduce network use, even at times when spare capacity is vastly available. It also may not optimise the need for network reinforcement. To address precisely this, charges may instead scale with users' contribution to overall network peak. This means that they are linked to the capacity utilised at the time of network peak load. Compared to individual peak, this approach reflects better how users' behaviour relates to grid cost. Network users benefit from reducing withdrawal or injection when the network is heavily utilised. Their reduction of network use during those times avoids costly expansion (cf. Crew et al., 1995). However, overall network peak is more difficult to predict and thus it is more complicated for an individual user to reduce coincident peak utilisation and control her network charges.

Similar to the various types of capacity components, there are several options to design volumetric or energy-based charges. Volumetric charges are based on a user's energy exchanged with the grid. They may be charged to consumers or generators as well as to both in combination. Consumers are usually charged for monthly or yearly withdrawal whereas generators are charged for injections in the same period. Network operators can predetermine the shares of cost to be recovered from a particular user group. Alternatively, with locationally differentiated tariffs, the cost split may emerge from the dominant grid use. For example, generators would pay in exporting areas while in the load dominated parts of the grid consumers are charged. When generation and consumption are rather homogeneous, the actual cost split makes no difference as generators would symmetrically pass on any charges they face to their consumers. However, in a more diverse energy system, passing cost on to consumers may reduce some generators' competitiveness or may affect some consumers more than others. Under such circumstances, an adequate cost split between injections and withdrawal becomes critical for efficient energy systems.

For network users who withdraw energy from but also feed energy into the grid—i.e., prosumers—charges may be netted over a certain period. Such net withdrawal is easy to assess with simple types of metering devices. Additionally, this approach provides an opportunity to support distributed generation in immediate proximity to consumption. If prices for energy supplied from the distribution grid exceed the remuneration for energy fed into the grid, prosumers gain from having their withdrawal netted over a preferably long period. This means that part of the electricity that is actually withdrawn from the grid, is not metered or billed for, as it evens out with injections during the netting period. This is illustrated in Fig. 4.1. However, if prosumers gain too much by exporting to the grid, injections may add up to a new, higher network peak and cause expensive transformer upgrades. With charges based on net withdrawal, prosumers network bills reduce disproportionately to their reduction of grid use and thus do not adequately reflect the cost they cause.

Increasingly, network charges are differentiated concerning time and location. Network utilisation varies over time and correspondingly capacity—as well as energy-based charges may vary over time too. Examples can be found in seasonal tariffs, differentiation between weekdays and weekends, up until hourly price windows. Real-time pricing on

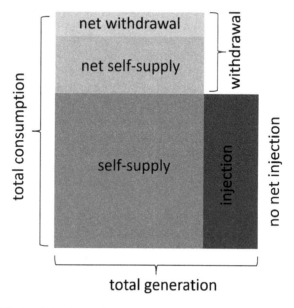

Fig. 4.1 Netting injection and withdrawal for prosumers (*Source* authors based on Brandstätt [2021a])

the other hand, is not yet very established for electricity distribution networks. Network operators and regulators often set charges uniformly irrespective of network users' location or of distance between injection and withdrawal. Yet, network cost may vary significantly between, for example, urban and rural areas, as well as between generation- or demand-dominated parts of the grid, thus potentially justifying locational differentiation. Another form of locational differentiation is between higher and lower voltage levels. Historically, electricity was supplied from central plants at higher grid levels and thus cost is passed down in a cascade from higher to lower grid levels (Brandstätt et al., 2015). This means that consumption at lower voltage would utilise all higher voltage assets while for consumption at higher voltage the remaining grid at lower voltage is not necessary. Therefore, network tariffs could be lower at high or medium voltage compared with low-voltage levels. With distributed generation, however, electricity for users at higher voltage might be provided at the lowest voltage levels given the possibility of reverse flows or bidirectional flows. This changes the way network charges are linked to different levels but does not affect the reasoning for differentiation.

4.3 Challenges and Trends in Network Access in the Presence of Decentralisation and Decarbonisation

Network charges have traditionally primarily served to finance and thereby sustain the grid. However, during the energy transition era, in addition to financing, they are increasingly required to provide adequate signals for coordination within the system. In accordance with common challenges in distribution grids today, in the following we discuss potentially adequate network charges for distributed generation, prosumers, and for flexible consumers and relate them to current developments such as unbundling, smart metering and aggregation.

Historically, distribution systems served small- to medium-sized consumers receiving their electricity from central generation at higher grid levels. Now, increasingly, generation is distributed according to availability of renewable energy sources. Distributed generations are often located in proximity to consumers in distribution grids. Electricity supply is decentralising and therefore distribution grids are an increasingly critical infrastructure for the energy transition. Distribution networks are challenged with integrating new, active network users. Regular private consumers and conventional businesses are rather inflexible and passive users. As electricity systems transition to a net-zero-carbon future, we increasingly see the rise of users with flexible appliances, electric vehicles, or electric heating systems. In many countries, it has also become standard for medium-sized enterprises to manage their energy demands and coordinate with electricity system needs. Consequently, they can participate in makers for balancing and grid frequency regulation services. Unless the network operator has the power and resources to actively control all these users, price signals from network charges or flexibility markets can be a way to achieve this participation. The latter will be discussed in more detail in Chapter 6. It should be noted that network tariffs inevitably provide new network users with incentives of some sorts. Yet, if tariffs are not designed for coordination, users are ill-directed and may even place considerable strain on the network rather than simply not contributing to the efficient operation and development of the grid.

Distributed generators (DGs) are among the first new network users in an energy transition. They enter the electricity market with an innovative technology and as competitors to established incumbents. Therefore, they are often subsidised and potentially exempted from network charges partially or totally. Such lower network charges for these users can be justified when generation is in proximity to consumers because it requires less network capacity than central generation to supply end consumers. However, too much distribution generation may reverse electricity flows in a network area such that further grid capacity is needed to transport distributed generation to other areas. The output of DGs is often fluctuating but not necessarily in the same way as demand. For example, during the night times, there might not be sufficient local consumption to match DG's production thus requiring transport capacity. Lastly, investment in DG is often most feasible in remote locations where it might cause significant network reinforcement. Thus, exempting distributed generation from network charges under all conditions might lead to inefficient utilisation and development of network capacity. To integrate distributed generation efficiently, connection charges need to reflect local differences within the grid. Network charges that signal the need for future network expansion will steer distributed generators to locate near a consumption type that matches their output.

For prosumers, DG is in highest possible proximity to consumption and consequently they save on volumetric network charges for energy supplied onsite rather than withdrawn from the grid. Yet, if the main consumption peak does not coincide with local generation, required network capacity and corresponding cost remain largely unchanged. Thus, distribution grids may lose revenues and be forced to raise tariffs for all consumers due to prosumption (i.e., the act of production by consumers) (Brandstätt, 2021a; cf. Felder & Athawale, 2014). Consequently, the incentive for self-supply increases and more consumers will consider onsite generation. These unintended effects are exacerbated when volumetric charges are based on net withdrawal and thereby encourage even more of the demand reduction. Efficient charges for self-supply, therefore, might involve incorporating non-volumetric components to account for the remaining capacity requirement. Alternatively, volumetric charges should reflect the actual time of use and thus recover the higher cost during network peak time.

Flexible users may also challenge existing network tariff schemes. First, when the tariff structure is uniform and flat, potentially flexible users have no incentives to utilise their flexibility to the benefit of themselves and the network. In fact, when incentives are non-existent or inadequate, investments in flexibility might not even occur and demand could remain more inelastic. In contrast, when the price signal is efficient (such as dynamic pricing), investment in flexibility can happen as network users can use their flexibility to optimise their network bill based on the tariffs they are faced with (Brandstätt, 2021c; cf. Horau & Perez, 2019).

Second, flexible resources, such as electric vehicles, will not be optimised at all under volumetric charges. Switching at least partially to capacity-based charges, on the other hand, nudges some flattening of the load curve. Yet, when the network is not congested and excess local generation is available, charges should ideally incentivise or at least do not penalise if electric vehicles match this supply and incur a peak in the load curve. Therefore, locationally and temporally differentiated charges might outperform uniform capacity-based charges for electric vehicles.

When applying to connect to the grid, new generators and additional demands may face scarcity and delays. Network operators are increasingly handling this based on price signals. For example, new network users may be able to obtain a quicker and potentially cheaper connection by accepting non-firm access to network capacity. Network operators increasingly retain the right to curtail renewable generation during peak hours, up to a certain percentage, or on the basis of some sort of compensation (see, for example, Furusawa et al., 2019). Similarly, flexible consumers can, in some countries, become connected to the grid at lower charges for interruptible access. Essentially, this adds firmness as another dimension of access to temporal and locational differentiation. We will discuss this further in Chapter 5. Also, such arrangements exhibit a mix between price incentives from network charges and active control by the network operator.

In many countries unbundling rules now separate the different elements in the electricity value chain. Traditionally, electricity was supplied by a public utility company that owned and operated the entire network, generation, and retail businesses. Therefore, the industry market structure was monopolistic. In a quest to contain monopoly power, increase efficiency, and foster innovation, the core monopoly realm of power grid is now often unbundled from the rest of the supply chain. (For more detail on this, see Chapter 8.) Particularly, distributed generators and other new technologies benefit from unbundling when entering the electricity market competing against established incumbents. Yet, the separation of network and supply can hamper efficient coordination along the value chain. For example, siting decisions for distributed generators between remote and more central locations has implications for the necessary network reinforcement. In the absence of firm internal organisation under an integrated monopoly, other mechanisms are needed to incentivise network users to consider the effects of their decisions on the network.

Network charges play a critical role for coordination in unbundled and decentralised systems. With an integrated electricity distribution, the integrated utility's corporate policies coordinate generation activities with the network business. The integrated utility's bundled price provides a signal to consumers about overall supply costs, including generation and the network. In unbundled systems on the other hand, network charges exist in parallel to prices from wholesale or flexibility markets. Network users take both cost components into account when operating their facilities or planning new investments. For a specific network user, the signals from electricity markets and network charges may well be conflicting in times. For example, low wholesale electricity prices on a sunny afternoon may coincide with high network charges during early afternoon peak time. Conflicting signals, however, are not necessarily inefficient. If consuming renewable electricity when it is abundant risks overloading the grid, high network charges may righteously overrule low wholesale prices. Ideally, network charges and other price signals interact efficiently to guide the access to electricity systems. However, as discussed earlier, network charges often do not efficiently signal the cost of network use but instead accommodate several other goals. As a result, they are mainly designed to be simple, more predictable, and transparent rather than necessarily efficient. Yet, incorporating other goals into network price signals can hinder the efficient coordination between the regulated distribution network and the rest of the electricity value chain.

With smart metering and aggregation, we observe two trends in distribution grids that can affect network charges and enable them to live up to the requirement of coordinating and integrating system users in a net-zero future. Firstly, network charges are becoming increasingly targeted and differentiated and, secondly, access regimes to distribution networks increasingly incorporate restrictions according to scarcity and valuation of the respective capacity. This differentiation of tariffs is enabled and facilitated by new stakeholders and innovative technology.

Smart meters, for example, source the information on individual network use that is necessary to bill the grid use in dimensions which drive the cost. With advanced meters, network operators can now charge, for example, for network use during peak times without causing large transaction cost to network operators or users. These innovative meters also provide information to network operators about the potential flexibility that individual network users hold. Network users, on the other hand, obtain information about aspects of their operational decisions that drive their network charges. Thereby they have the opportunity to align the gain they derive from utilising the grid with the cost they cause.

The other important factor is the rise of aggregators. Aggregation, as a new role within the energy system, helps users market their flexibility within what may seem a maze of price incentives from different markets and tariff schemes. Aggregation is also usually accompanied with automation as relying on active participation by individual owners of flexible resources might not be realistic. Flexibility from electric vehicles, for example, is often questioned based on the fact that vehicle owners prefer the comfort of simply plugging in their vehicle when arriving. Planning and optimising the charging or use of appliances like a washing machine or dryer seems too much effort for household customers. However, with new technologies small and uninvolved users can simply hand over their potential flexibility to an aggregator and earn a small saving without having to get involved in trading and optimisation themselves. Particularly, at the distribution level, where many users do not have the skills or interest to engage with the network or with energy markets, aggregators potentially buffer the complexity of differentiated tariffs and their interaction with other market signals for uninvolved network users.

Lastly, the role of the network operator is evolving from mere provision of transport and distribution infrastructure to the provision of a platform for information and services within an integrated energy system (cf. Brandstätt et al., 2016). It is possible that in such a transformed role, network operators can also access new streams of revenues and thus reduce the need to finance the infrastructure, particularly new, smart assets, solely from network users. Think of aggregated, timely information on the state of a certain network area, which can be useful to stakeholders marketing energy and flexibility. Such information is sourced from communicating network equipment which is otherwise needed for maintaining stability and operational security of the grid. With the additional revenue stream from flexibility providers, the cost for the innovative equipment does not need to be recovered solely from network users. What proportion of cost to assign to such new stakeholders and how to raise this additional revenue efficiently and in an accepted way is currently still a topic for further research.

4.4 Conclusions

Network charges are a means both to finance network infrastructure as well as to coordinate network users with the grid. In distribution grids during transition towards a net-zero future, network charges are required to not only raise more revenue but also to raise it differently in order to integrate new network users. The challenge of integrating new users at the distribution network level differs for generation, prosumers, and flexible and active users.

Network operators have a large toolbox of different types of network charges on their hands to meet this challenge. The traditional distinction is between one-off charges for connection and continuous charges for network usage. Cost-reflective charges enable network users to balance the gain they obtain from accessing and utilising the network, with the cost that their operation and investments cause in the grid. Assessing network cost in relation to network use, however, is not a trivial task. For different tariff options various components need to be determined such as deep vs shallow costs, fixed vs variable costs and general versus user-specific costs. A typical three-part tariff, therefore, includes charging components such as fixed, capacity-, or load-based as well as components based on energy volumes. Weights among the pricing parts for network charges are often determined according to non-economic criteria such as simplicity, predictability, and user acceptance. A similar balance is to be struck for different degrees of time and locational differentiation of network access as well as restrictions concerning firmness and flexibility.

In general, differentiated tariffs tend to be more efficient in coordinating diverse network users with a high propensity for adapting their demand according to price signals. Yet, differentiation generally entails transaction cost both on the side of network users as well as for the network operator. The rise of smart metering devices as well as the evolution of aggregation as a role in distribution grids facilitate efficient tariffs by buffering unprepared network users from undue complexity.

A trend towards more temporally and locationally differentiated tariffs can already be observed in some countries. Furthermore, concepts such as curtailable network access and buy-back of access in flexibility markets lay out the path for further differentiation. These will be discussed in more detail in the following two chapters.

References

ACER. (2021). *Report on distribution tariff methodologies in Europe.* http://www.acer.europa.eu/Official_documents/Acts_of_the_Agency/Publication/ACER%20Report%20on%20D-Tariff%20Methodologies.pdf

Bonbright, J. C. (1961). *The principles of public utility rates.* Columbia University Press.

Brandstätt, C. (2021a). *Network charging schemes and self-supply: Instruments to prevent self-reinforcing dynamics* (Bremen Energy Working Papers, No. 36). Jacobs University Bremen.

Brandstätt, C. (2021b). Note on the efficiency of peak load pricing. *mimeo.*

Brandstätt, C. (2021c). The efficiency of peak-load pricing in electricity networks with investments into self-supply and electrification. *mimeo.*

Brandstätt, C., & Poudineh, R. (2020). Rethinking the network access regime: The case for differentiated and tradeable access rights. *Oxford Energy Forum, 124,* 24–28.

Brandstätt, C., Brunekreeft, G., Buchmann, M., & Friedrichsen, N. (2016). Balancing between competition and coordination in smart grids—A Common Information Platform (CIP). *Economics of Energy & Environmental Policy, 6*(1), 93–109.

Brandstätt, C., Brunekreeft, G., Furusawa, K., & Hattori, T. (2015). *Distribution planning and pricing in view of increasing shares of intermittent, renewable energy in Germany and Japan* (Bremen Energy Working Papers, No. 20). Jacobs University Bremen.

CEER. (2020). *CEER Paper on Electricity Distribution Tariffs Supporting the Energy Transition* (Ref: C19-DS-55-04). Distribution Systems Working Group. https://www.ceer.eu/documents/104400/-/-/fd5890e1-894e-0a7a-21d9-fa22b6ec9da0

Clastres, C., Percebois, J., Rabenaque, O., & Solier, B. (2019). Cross subsidies across electricity network users from renewable self-consumption. *Utilities Policy, 59*, 100925.

Crew, M. A., Fernando, C. S., & Kleindorfer, P. R. (1995). The theory of peak-load pricing: A survey. *Journal of Regulatory Economics, 8*, 215–248.

Edison Electric Institute. (2013). *Disruptive challenges: Financial implications and strategic responses to a changing retail electric business*. Washington. http://roedel.faculty.asu.edu/PVGdocs/EEI-2013-report.pdf

Eurostat. (2020). *Energy prices and costs in Europe* (Report, SWD(2020)951). https://eur-lex.europa.eu/legal-content/EN/TXT/PDF/?uri=CELEX:52020DC0951&from=EN

Felder, F. A., & Athawale, R. (2014). The life and death of the utility death spiral. *Electricity Journal, 27*, 9–16.

Furusawa, K., Brunekreeft, G., & Hattori, T. (2019). *Constrained connection for distributed generation by DSOs in European countries* (Bremen Energy Working Papers, No. 28).

Horau, Q., & Perez, Y. (2019). Network tariff design with prosumers and electromobility: Who wins, who loses? *Energy Economics, 83*, 26–39.

Neuteleers, S., Mulder, M., & Hindriks, F. (2017). Assessing fairness of dynamic grid tariffs. *Energy Policy, 108*, 111–120.

Richardson, D. B. (2013). Electric vehicles and the electric grid: A review of modeling approaches. impacts, and renewable energy integration. *Renewable and Sustainable Energy Reviews, 19*, 247–254.

Simshauser, P. (2016). Distribution network prices and solar PV: Resolving rate instability and wealth transfers through demand tariffs. *Energy Economics, 54*, 108–122.

CHAPTER 5

Improving Efficiency: Flexible Network Access Regime and Auction for Allocation of Network Capacity

Abstract This chapter looks at the efficient allocation of access to existing and future grid capacity. The analysis departs from the concept of restricted rather than universal network access and introduces options of assigning access rights via auctions against offering them at regulated prices. It connects recent developments towards selectively restricting access rights as well as increasingly common practices of network operators buying back access rights from users by compensating them for access restrictions. Schemes that distinguish between different dimensions of access, rather than correcting the initial allocation are the consequential next step towards a net-zero-carbon future. Efficient approaches for the assignment of access enable the system operator to alleviate existing constraints and help to avoid grid expansion in situations where coordination mechanisms can manage the grid.

Keywords Network access regime · Flexible network access · Auction for network capacity

© The Author(s), under exclusive license to Springer Nature Switzerland AG 2022
R. Poudineh et al., *Electricity Distribution Networks in the Decentralisation Era*,
https://doi.org/10.1007/978-3-030-98069-6_5

5.1 Introduction

Grid access is a vital requirement for generators, consumers, and to exchange energy with others remotely. When grid capacity is scarce—i.e., when the network is congested—users cannot access it to the full extent they desire. This means that in view of congestion, access to the grid needs to be restricted to match network capacity. This chapter investigates different mechanisms for restricting and managing network access and discusses their relevance in a decarbonised distribution system.[1]

Congestion is becoming more and more important in distribution grids due to increasing loads and techno-economic challenges of network capacity expansion. Historically, distribution grids were designed to distribute centrally generated electricity to dispersed and passive consumers. Accordingly, distribution grids were usually dimensioned to cater to end users' maximum demand. Distributed generations such as wind and solar power have significantly altered network loads and are often the cause for grid reinforcement. Similarly, newly electrified energy demands for heating and transportation services are expected to create the need for network expansion in, at least, parts of the distribution grid. In many cases however, network expansion is not the most straightforward option. On the one hand, it can be quite expensive, especially in distribution grids where, at lower voltage levels, lines are often underground. On the other hand, new infrastructure is often faced with public opposition for constituting an intervention in the natural environment.

Given the cost of network reinforcement and low public acceptance of new infrastructure, congestion is increasingly managed rather than eliminated. This requires adequate mechanisms to allocate access to scarce network capacity. Managing congestion means assigning access to a certain user at a given point and time. Access rights entitle the holder to using and benefiting from network capacity. Different types of users gain to varying degrees from network access. In economic terms, they obtain different utility from being able to use the grid. These differences impact the priority with which network users should be connected or curtailed.

For example, a new wind generator seeking to connect in a constrained part of the grid may cause congestion, when the current capacity has

---

[1] The chapter is loosely based on several other publications on the topic by the authors of this book, in particular Brandstätt and Poudineh (2020, 2021).

already been assigned entirely to existing generators. As a result, connection of this new generator is delayed. Given that wind generation is intermittent, already connected generators likely do not always utilise their access capacity fully. Looking from an efficiency perspective, the existing capacity available to incumbents can be shared with the new generator. Yet, as generation profiles are likely very similar, an allocation mechanism and incentives to invest in intermediary storage are needed to organise collective optimal use of the network. This can be a temporary solution until additional capacity becomes available. Depending on value added from new generation and cost of congestion management versus additional network capacity, efficient allocation may even render expansion obsolete altogether.

The same applies to additional demands from other users such as electric vehicles. Charging electric vehicles increases the maximum load of households or commercial buildings significantly. Especially, when the number of charging points within a certain area grows, it can cause scarcity and require expansion. Yet, charging can also be coordinated to make optimal use of the existing grid and thus increase utilisation rather than maximum load. An adequate allocation of access rights ensures this coordination.

Initially, access rights originate from the network owner who built the capacity and are assigned by a network or system operator. System operation can lie in the hands of the network owner or in those of an independent or a collective institution. Either way, assigning access rights requires overseeing the availability of existing capacity as well as network users' demand for capacity. Access rights can be universal or restricted in certain dimensions (for example locationally, temporally, and regarding firmness) and mechanisms to allocate them can be administrative or market-based. To inform an opinion on how best to design both access rights and the mechanisms to allocate them in order to meet the challenges related to the energy transition, in what follows, this chapter

- provides an overview of different forms of access,
- discusses different types of access right allocations, and
- relates them to the challenges for distribution networks in decarbonisation era.

5.2 Forms of Access

Access rights are a means to coordinate the demand for network capacity and its availability. Thus, the dimensions of access assigned by the system operator should match the dimensions in which demand and availability vary. While universal access represents an option to access in any dimension, i.e., for example at any time or location, rights to restricted access specify the precise type of access that users are entitled to and that network operators need to cater for. Users can substitute universal access for restricted, but not without losing some comfort or benefit, and hence they are likely willing to pay less for restricted than for universal access. For network operators, restricted access can be provided cheaper as it is more predictable and reliable.

Historically, access rights to the network have often been universal and tiered only according to the size of a user's grid connection—i.e., according to the fuse size. Yet, for most users, demand profiles vary over time and it is widely understood that a heavily utilised connection often requires significantly more reinforcement than one which is likely to remain idle regularly. From the network's perspective, the maximum load determines how much capacity is required. However, individual loads even out if they do not occur simultaneously. Conversely, the sum of access rights can exceed the maximum capacity in a single dimension, depending on the specification of access and expected utilisation. The quantity of access can be defined as power or energy volume.[2] While, from a system operator perspective, capacity or load is a naturally relevant dimension, users often prefer the concept of being entitled to a certain quantity of energy for withdrawal or injection over time (cf. Xu, 2019). In European distribution systems, access prices are shifting towards power (i.e., per kW) as the charging parameter. Most member states of the EU charge, at least partially, per connected capacity for establishing access initially and the number of states that base recurring access prices on load is on the rise (ACER, 2021). For more details on network tariffs, see also Chapter 4.

In addition to the mere quantity of access allowance, access rights may vary in further dimensions such as direction, location, time, and firmness. When assigned access is limited to certain of these dimensions it is differentiated or restricted, rather than universal. Such differentiations are

---

[2] In fact, for sufficiently small time steps the difference becomes very small.

to facilitate coordination and efficient system development. Access or use which results in lower incremental cost are cheaper to cater for, and thus provide users with incentives to adjust their demand for capacity accordingly. This optimises network cost in line with the potential benefit users derive from the network, and thereby maximises efficiency.

The network can be accessed and utilised as withdrawal and injection. Generators and consumers need access in only one direction while batteries and prosumers require both, although never at the same time. Within a network, reverse directions can balance out to a certain extent, so that less capacity is required than the sum of individual access requests. Therefore, access for injection is provided at lower specific cost in networks with mainly demand. Catering for additional withdrawal in such networks is comparatively more expensive. To understand this, imagine a remote generation location and a load centre connected by a distribution line of fixed capacity. If access is universal for withdrawal or injection, the system operator can allocate rights according to the total capacity. However, when rights are restricted to generation or withdrawal respectively, the operator gets to assign additional rights according to the amount of access requests in the opposite direction.

Furthermore, the network is accessed in a specific grid area or at a certain location. Today, per default users often have access to the entire grid. With increasing decentralisation, however, access only to the immediate neighbourhood or local grid level is cheaper to provide. Most network users are tied to a specific location or area. Some new user types, such as electric vehicles, however, are locationally flexible and might benefit from locationally varying access rights. To see this, assume a photovoltaic generator feeding electricity into the grid in an urban area. If, for example, a transformer towards higher voltage levels is congested, additional universal access rights are not physically feasible. However, the system operator can still assign rights to access locally for the generator to supply consumers in the same grid area. In fact, if access rights do not match the locational granularity of demands, they are less likely to be fully used. When the beforementioned generator has universal access but supplies its neighbour, it will almost inevitably leave a part of allocated access rights unused. At the distribution level assigning locationally varying access is still rather uncommon, especially at the lowest voltage levels. However, in some member states of the European Union, for example, prices for access vary regionally (ACER, 2021). Additionally,

Austria and Portugal offer reduced prices for energy communities which locally share electricity (Bridge, 2019).

In practice, access rights are regularly time specific. Overall, users need to have access to the grid for the entire life span of their assets, which can be years or decades. The specific demand for access, however, may vary significantly within hours or even minutes. Access is generally more valuable during peak than during off-peak times and seasons. In colder countries, for example, it is lower during summer than during winter and vice versa in warmer countries. This means a network operator can assign double the amount of physically feasible universal access rights if half of the access is restricted to the peak and the other half to the off-peak. In fact, given that users' demand varies, universal access rights are likely to remain unused for part of the timespan they cover and thus inefficiently prevent others from accessing the idle capacity. Therefore, differentiating between day and night time is common for network operators in many countries. Grid-specific peak and off-peak periods are still less common, while some operators even consider seasonal differences. For a discussion on the European practice see, for example, ACER (2021). During peak periods, restricted access is increasingly common. In Germany, for example, renewable generation can be curtailed without compensation during peak times up to a certain threshold of overall yearly production (CEER, 2018).

Apart from quantity, location, and time, access rights can also be restricted with respect to firmness. Access rights define an option to use the network. Network capacity is needed only when this option is actually exercised. Historically, the network operator assumes, based on past experience and projections, that large numbers of users, such as households, do not use fully use this option at all times. This allows the operator to issue access rights for more capacity than is physically available. Given that indeed not all users fully exercise their access rights, more users overall benefit from access. However, whenever exercised access threatens to become physically unfeasible, the network operator needs to intervene and curtail or buy-back access. To facilitate this, access rights can also stipulate a certain level of utilisation by allowance or even control. Access rights that can be curtailed transfer control over network use from the user to the network operator. Thus, in view of some proportion of universal access, controllable or curtailable access can increase utilisation and reduce cost.

Furthermore, if access is universal and rights are exclusive, capacity assigned to one user may be blocked for others in some dimensions, even when it is not used. Exclusive access rights that do not match the temporal and locational granularity facilitate intentional withholding. When access rights span too large periods or network areas and load profiles vary temporally and locationally, system users will almost inevitably leave some part of their access rights unused.

Besides the ones discussed above, as system use evolves additional dimensions of network access may gain importance. Furthermore, differentiating based on multiple dimensions of network access at once may become efficient (e.g., injection at specific points for local transfer or controllable peak withdrawal). However, differentiation always comes with complexity and transaction cost for both network users and network operator. Thus, any additional degree of differentiation needs to be justified by expected gains for network users. Essentially, if a universal access option exists in parallel to cheaper restricted forms of access, users get to evaluate this trade-off for themselves. For the network operator on the other hand, offering additional forms of restricted access already entails some administrative effort and may require innovative technology.

5.3 Allocation of Access

Network operators or regulators can choose from a wide variety of mechanisms to assign access to existing, and particularly to congested capacity, as well as to potential future network capacity.

Efficient approaches for the assignment of access enable the system operator to alleviate existing constraints and ideally also help to refrain from grid expansion where instead coordination mechanisms can manage the grid equally effectively. Even when the investment decision is efficiently timed, congestion may arise when capacity is delayed. While the delay itself often cannot be prevented, efficient allocation of access should help to share and prioritise access to existing capacity according to how users value it. For example, when a new photovoltaic plant seeks connection in an area of the grid, where the existing capacity is already fully utilised by incumbent generators, network operators have two options to provide access for a new generator. One option is expanding network capacity and the other would be allocating access to existing capacity such that the new generator has access according to the value of additional feed-in. Even with expansion, however, an allocation mechanism that allows for sharing access to existing capacity will still be necessary, or at least beneficial, in order to efficiently bridge the gap until additional capacity becomes available. Efficient allocation, however, is only one concern. Other criteria such as complexity and transaction cost, reliability or fairness, and acceptability play a role as well.

Access to network capacity can be assigned implicitly—i.e., for example, it can follow from successful trading in the energy market. Alternatively, it can be assigned explicitly, when the network operator or regulator assigns rights administratively or in a market-based manner. Administrative allocation follows historically or logically motivated rules, as opposed to an allocation that forms in a market setting as a result of supply and demand. In practice, dedicated combinations of these approaches are common.

Traditionally, network access in distribution systems is often assigned administratively. A grandfathering approach ensures that all parties who had access in the past will continue to have access as the distribution system evolves. Connection queues administer new access requests on a first-come-first-served basis. In the spirit of a level playing field, network operators may also decide to assign access on a pro-rata basis, enabling minimum access for all connection-seeking parties. Another common administrative approach is to assign access to any user who is able and willing to pay a listed access price—i.e., a connection charge. Listed prices or network charges, however, exhibit market-based features if tariffs and access products are sufficiently differentiated. Efficient peak load prices according to Steiner (1957), for example, signal the long-term marginal cost of supplying access and in case of congestion also represent users' willingness to pay for access. Such prices, although difficult to implement in practice, essentially replicate the efficient outcome of a market.

With a fully market-based allocation, however, network users get to submit their demand in a market environment where it is matched with the corresponding supply of access capacity. Such fully market-based approaches to assigning access link the allocation of access rights to an auction or negotiation. An explicit allocation occurs in the form of contracts that grant users access (cf. e.g., Hogan, 1992; Oren, 1997). Alternatively, access rights can be assigned implicitly or passively based on the outcome of an energy market down- or upstream of the network (cf. e.g., Green, 2007; Schweppe et al., 1988). The differentiation of access rights is tied to the design of these markets. In a zonal or nodal market, for example, the assigned access rights are locationally differentiated. At the distribution level, these market designs are still quite uncommon. Instead, in a single price, congestion-blind electricity market design initially assigned access is universal.

If energy is traded over a large area and long periods—i.e., with rather universal access rights, the outcome of the initial allocation can be improved via reallocation of more granular access. Therefore, network operators engage in redispatch or curtailment when congestion emerges based on the initially allocated access rights. Absent a correction of physically unfeasible rights, system reliability is at risk. When, on the other hand, unused access rights are not reallocated, capacity may remain unutilised or even be strategically withheld. As network users compete in electricity markets based on their access to the network capacity, some users may see it beneficial to hold on to access rights despite not intending to use them, simply in order to prevent competitors from down- or upstream trading.

Mechanisms to correct an inefficient or even unfeasible initial allocation can be administrative even if the initial allocation was market-based and vice versa. An example for administrative reallocation is a simple curtailment rule, such as first-come-first-served or pro-rata curtailment. If curtailment is compensated and the compensation relates to users' cost or their forgone benefits, the originally administrative measure becomes more market-based. Similarly, cost-based redispatch, where the network operator assesses network users' marginal cost and redispatches accordingly, represents a more, but not fully, market-based approach. In market-based-redispatch network users submit their bids for countertrade to the network operator who then reallocates their access rights according to the merit order. This essentially corresponds to buying back unfeasible access rights and allocating new feasible ones instead. As compared to the cost-based approach a well-designed auction potentially bridges the information gap between network operator and network user concerning the cost of reallocation (cf. Brandstätt & Poudineh, 2021). Lastly, market-based reallocation of access rights could also occur among network users, with the network operator merely overseeing their trades to ensure system reliability.

In the case of a congestion-blind electricity market, initially all electricity sales from distributed generators in a constrained grid area are accepted and thereby implicitly granted access to the grid. However, given that there are constraints, some of those trades are physically unfeasible.

This means the network operator needs to make sure that less energy is fed into the grid. Therefore, it can either curtail one, for example the most expensive one, of the generators or potentially limit feed-in partially for all of them. In this example, the design options discussed above determine how to select which generator to curtail and how to compensate the intervention. The European Union, for example, prescribes a market-based redispatch, to replace historically evolved administrative mechanisms such as cost-based redispatch or last-in-first-out curtailment[3] (EC, 2019).

It is intuitive that administrative allocation of grid access is not necessarily efficient since it is either not linked or insufficiently linked to the benefits that network users derive from the access and to the cost of providing capacity. The virtue of administrative mechanisms is instead that they are simple, transparent and relatively reliable. Auctions on the other hand, potentially allocate access efficiently. Their main promise compared to expert projections based on network operators experience, is the revelation of information concerning the demand for network capacity. Yet, there are many concerns regarding a fully market-based allocation of access, such as concerning transaction cost and complexity (e.g., Stern & Turvey, 2003), as well as about buying power towards the network operator and limited liquidity (e.g., Helm, 2003; Newbery, 2003). In general, auctions are susceptive to strategic behaviour. Network users can benefit from limited liquidity or the potential for collusion in distribution grids and this is likely exacerbated with differentiated access to network capacity. Additionally, incentives for predatory behaviour arise as access rights are a precondition to compete in wholesale or retail markets for electricity. Adequate market design is crucial to overcome these challenges of market-based allocation. Theoretically, the different design options for auctions are seemingly endless and it is therefore tempting to assume that network access could be auctioned efficiently.

In distribution systems the initial allocation of access rights usually occurs upon connection for the entire lifespan of an asset. Initially assigned access can be reallocated as actual utilisation is revealed or as the system evolves and becomes more congested. Such reallocation can occur

---

[3] This means, for example, that if several generators cause congestion of a particular asset, the one with the most recent connection has to reduce injections to alleviate the constraint.

in the form of curtailment, redispatch, and countertrading.[4] Alternatively, where congestion is expected, we increasingly see network operators initially assigning restricted access rights, in order to facilitate or limit the need for managing congestion closer to time of delivery. For interconnectors at the transmission level, market-based allocation of access to network capacity is common. However, this is not (yet) the case for distribution grids. Yet, at distribution levels, the first implementations of markets for flexibility or congestion management are taking place as well. This will be discussed in more detail in the next chapter (6) on flexibility markets.

5.4 Challenges and Trends

Allocating network access efficiently enables the system operator to mitigate existing constraints and ideally also to refrain from grid expansion to the extent that allocation can manage capacity scarcity. Historically, access has been assigned in relatively broad dimensions and predominantly administratively. However, in view of growing demand for network capacity and of increasingly flexible network users, new approaches to allocating network access emerge.

Firstly, access rights are assigned in increasingly differentiated dimensions. As users are becoming more flexible, they are able to optimise the benefit they obtain from different types of access. An electric vehicle fleet for example benefits from being able to choose between accessing the grid for charging immediately versus charging later with cheaper access rights. Similarly, new generators potentially locate in a less congested part of the grid, when access there comes at a lower cost or higher firmness—i.e., with a lower risk of curtailment. In distribution systems today, we observe a growing diversity of dimensions for access to suit a variety of user types and match system operators' various coordination needs.

Secondly, the allocation of access rights departs from simple administrative approaches and increasingly tends to follow market principles. As demands for heat or transportation are electrified, electricity networks are expanded and thus become more expensive. With the increasing cost, the focus widens from mere system stability to economic efficiency. While the

---

[4] Redispatch and countertrading are closely related, and the terms are often used interchangeably. Redispatch mostly refers to when a system operator initiates specific deviations from users' planned operation schedules, whereas countertrading generally means the market-based acquisition of constraint alleviation.

former is covered well by simple administrative approaches, the latter goal points towards marked-based solutions. In a setting where several wind generators congest a distribution link to the demand centre, curtailing all generators at the same rate or curtailing first those generators that connected last, resolves congestion and restores technical reliability of the grid. However, in a market for access rights to the congested part of the grid, prices go up for injection and withdrawal becomes cheaper. This can incentivise local consumption from batteries, charging stations, or electrolysers and can potentially increase overall benefit alongside resolving congestion.

The potential gains from differentiated access and market-based allocation can also bring about some challenges, for example concerning reliability, complexity, acceptance, market power as well as their interaction with other markets and mechanisms.

Network operators are often concerned about the reliability of market-based allocation, especially close to delivery. Particularly for curtailment, network operators often prefer administrative approaches, in order to prevent that a smouldering response to market incentives jeopardises system stability. A well-functioning, developed market, however, can probably be relied upon for correcting access allocation and as the trends outlined above continue, network operators have the opportunity to gain positive experience. Additionally, an administrative approach can be maintained as a last resort option combining the targets of economic efficiency and reliability.

Another challenge is acceptance of new models by network users. In principle, individual acceptance of new access regimes is increased by choice. Thus, some users benefit from new access dimensions and therefore approve of differentiated access. Yet, those that do not, can still opt for the universal access that they are used to. However, the prices of broader access dimensions may increase while flexible users who prefer restricted access have cheaper options. This may be perceived as unfair notwithstanding the benefits. These could be that such an approach increases overall welfare and potentially limits the price increase for universal access without the efficiency gain from restricted options. Just like acceptance by network operators, user acceptance may build up over time and can be fostered by information and transparency (Neuteleers et al., 2017).

Increasing complexity is another issue connected to efficient allocation of network access. Especially, for uninvolved users, handling a myriad of access options on a recurring basis can be very demanding and likely outweighs their additional benefit by far. In economic terms, it entails preventive transaction cost. This challenge can be met in at least three ways. Firstly, as argued with regard to acceptance, broad and long-term access rights can remain available for uninvolved users alongside more intricate concepts of access for others. Thus, a small household would obtain universal access for an extended timespan whereas, heat pumps within a district heating system can optimise their access in several of the dimensions mentioned in Sect. 5.2 of this chapter. However, uninvolved users, albeit being small and inert, may collectively still harbour a significant flexibility potential. To harvest this potential, secondly, the transaction cost of handling different dimensions of access and a recurring market-based allocation is reduced significantly by new technologies such as smart meters and control interfaces. As these automate the procurement of access rights to a large extent, they effectively buffer the associated complexity. Aggregation represents a third solution to overcome the challenge of increased complexity. The evolution of access allocation gives rise to a new role within distributed energy systems. As market opportunities arise, we see third parties bundling the interests of small network users and effectively optimising them in view of incentives from the network and energy markets. This means that even when a household prefers simple and uninvolving grid access, retailers with some control options over larger numbers of network users, can provide this while still optimising access requirements to a certain extent and without limiting users expected benefits. Lastly, also system operators may face substantial additional effort, when offering and administering a variety of different access dimensions and organising or at least overseeing a market for access rights. Their transaction cost is also reduced by innovative technology and likely exhibits a steep learning potential. Yet, system operators' additional costs of allocating access more efficiently have to outweigh the benefit of reducing network cost and improving the service delivered to network users.

The interaction between market-based allocation of network access and other pricing or coordination mechanisms such as network tariffs as well as energy and flexibility markets may be challenging in practice too. If network users, or their aggregators adjust how they access and use the network with respect to their temporal and local flexibility, the access regime is only one factor in the overall optimisation. Network tariffs and energy or flexibility markets influence users' potential savings or profit from flexibility as well. Network tariffs potentially overlap with access allocation, especially as the line between connection and use-of-system becomes blurrier and as tariffs and access rights become increasingly time- and locationally differentiated. Yet, they also serve the additional purpose of financing the infrastructure. Consequently, they may distort and even superimpose the incentive from an access regime. Similarly, flexibility markets can be a platform for the network operator to reallocate access. Yet depending on the specific design, they can also be used by other market participants to optimise and balance their portfolio which can jeopardise an efficient access allocation. Energy prices, on the other hand, ideally allocate energy efficiently alongside network capacity. In theory, all mechanisms can interact efficiently and complementarily lead to an overall efficient outcome. However, they all need to be designed carefully, to prevent distortions upon their interaction.

Lastly, as with any market-based allocation, the allocation of access rights is potentially affected by market power. In theory, both network operator and network users may act strategically in a market for access rights and thereby impair the overall efficient outcome. Strategy for the network operator is primarily linked to the monopoly of the network and ideally addressed by regulation (cf. Chapter 8). However, in addition network operators are traditionally in charge of system reliability. Therefore, they have a strong incentive to reserve some capacity in excess or retain a certain amount of flexibility. This is because the network operator or regulator is likely held responsible for system failure even if it is the result of strategic and reckless bidding strategies from network users (see, for example, Newbery, 2003). This strengthens the position of network users in an auction market, especially when there are no alternative reliability mechanisms (for example, as proposed in Billimoria & Poudineh, 2019).

The strategic interests for network users are mainly to obtain access cheaply and to prevent access for up- or downstream competitors. First, the motivation to shade bids or understate demand is rooted in uncertainty about competing bids and about the value of a particular access right. If network users reveal their own willingness to pay when others would bid less, they risk paying more than necessary to obtain the access they desire. Optimally they would bid just slightly above their closest competitor. Yet, if they guess this price, they risk that they may not win the access rights they need. On the other hand, if the value of access rights is uncertain because it also depends on what benefit they enable for others, users who estimate the value most optimistically will gain access to the grid. In fact, winning the auction precisely reveals that the bid was (too) optimistic, thus cursing the win. Consequently, when buying access in an auction, network users generally have an incentive to understate their demand.

Predatory behaviour is another potential strategy. Incumbent network users and other strong bidders may attempt to secure access to capacity simply in order to prevent that others can compete with them in the network-based markets such as wholesale and retail. When a generator, for example, buys access to a constrained part of the grid, it can obtain a higher revenue from selling his electricity in the constrained market, given that it can withhold network capacity. The revenue of the withholding generator is therefore higher than if a competitor had access and was able to drive down prices. Similarly, when an incumbent controls all existing network capacity, new generators are prevented from competing with them in the electricity market. Consequently, generators who withhold access rights, may be able to increase their profits in a therefore less-competitive electricity market. Initially they may lose revenue as they need to bid aggressively for access rights or may win more capacity than needed. However, this would be compensated for, when they are able to obtain additional profit from a dominant position in the electricity market.

In distribution systems competition may well be slim and network users may be able to learn from experience what their position in the market is. Over time, they could even exchange signals with their competitors. Yet, in practice, such strategies may be less relevant in distribution grids with intermittent and uninvolved users for whom strategic dispatch is either technically not possible or prevented by transaction cost (cf. Green & Vasilakos, 2010). If aggregators coordinate users, however, strategic behaviour may become more relevant in the future. In any case, careful and adequate market design as well as dedicated regulation can likely meet the challenge of market power and thus limit or even prevent strategic behaviour.

5.5 Conclusion

As congestion is becoming more relevant in decarbonised distribution systems, access regimes which are at the core of allocating scarce network capacity become increasingly important. Access rights may vary not only regarding the mere quantity of access allowance, but increasingly also with respect to direction, location, time, and firmness. Network operators or regulators can choose from a variety of different administrative or market-based mechanisms to assign access to network capacity.

Differentiation of network access and market design facilitate coordination and efficient system development. An access right which results in a lower incremental cost is cheaper to cater for, and thus provides users with incentives to adjust their demand for capacity accordingly. This optimises network costs in line with the potential benefit users derive from the network. Thus, efficient grid capacity allocation through access differentiation and the use of market mechanism can mitigate existing constraints and ideally also replace grid expansion where allocation manages capacity scarcity.

The potential gains from differentiated access and market-based allocation are accompanied with new challenges, for example concerning reliability, complexity, acceptance, market power as well as their interaction with other markets and mechanisms. These can potentially be overcome by adequate design of market rules, new roles, and smart technologies.

REFERENCES

ACER. (2021, February). *Report on distribution tariff methodologies in Europe*. Accessed on 27 March 2021 at https://www.acer.europa.eu/Official_doc uments/Acts_of_the_Agency/Publication/ACER%20Report%20on%20D-Tar iff%20Methodologies.pdf

Billimoria, F., & Poudineh, R. (2019). Market design for resource adequacy: A reliability insurance overlay on energy-only electricity markets. *Utilities Policy, 60*, art. 100935.

Brandstätt, C., & Poudineh, R. (2020). Rethinking the network access regime: The case for differentiated and tradeable access rights. *Oxford Energy Forum, 124*, 24–28.

Brandstätt, C., & Poudineh, R. (2021, July). *Market-based allocation and differentiation of access rights to network capacity in distribution grids* (OIES Papers, EL 45).

Bridge. (2019, December). *Energy Communities in the EU* (Report). Accessed on 27 March 2021 at https://www.h2020-bridge.eu/wp-content/uploads/2020/01/D3.12.d_BRIDGE_Energy-Communities-in-the-EU-2.pdf

CEER. (2018, December). *Status Review of Renewable Support Schemes in Europe for 2016 and 2017* (Report). Accessed on 27 March 2021 at https://www.ceer.eu/documents/104400/-/-/80ff3127-8328-52c3-4d01-0acbdb2d3bed

EC. (2019). Regulation 2019/943 of the European Parliament and of the council of 5 June 2019 on the internal market for electricity.

Green, R. (2007). Nodal pricing of electricity: How much does it cost to get it wrong? *Journal of Regulatory Economics, 31*, 125–149.

Green, R., & Vasilakos, N. (2010). Market behaviour with large amounts of intermittent generation. *Energy Policy, 38*(7), 3211–3220.

Helm, D. (2003). Auctions and energy networks. *Utilities Policy, 11*(1), 21–25.

Hogan, W. W. (1992). Contract networks for electric power transmission. *Journal of Regulatory Economics, 4*(2), 211–242.

Neuteleers, S., Mulder, M., & Hindriks, F. (2017). Assessing fairness of dynamic grid tariffs. *Energy Policy, 108*, 111–120.

Newbery, D. M. (2003). Network capacity auctions: Promise and problems. *Utilities Policy, 11*(1), 27–32.

Oren, S. S. (1997). Economic inefficiency of passive transmission rights in congested electricity systems with competitive generation. *Energy Journal, 18*(1), 63–83.

Schweppe, F. C., Caramanis, M. C., Tabors, R. D., & Bohn, R. E. (1988). *Spot pricing of electricity*. Kluwer Academic Publishers.

Steiner, P. O. (1957). Peak loads and efficient pricing. *Quarterly Journal of Economics, 71*(4), 585–610.

Stern, J., & Turvey, R. (2003). Auctions of capacity in network industries. *Utilities Policy, 11*(1), 1–8.

Xu, Z. (2019). *The electricity market design for decentralized flexibility sources* (OIES Paper EL 39). Oxford Institute for Energy Studies.

CHAPTER 6

Local Markets for Decentralised Flexibility Services

Abstract This chapter provides an overview of different concepts for local and decentralised markets for flexibility services. It distinguishes between network operators' need for flexibility to manage scarcity and capacity development and a corresponding market demand for flexibility to balance trading portfolios. Furthermore, it discusses product and market design touching upon differentiation, control option, prequalification, and illustrates them with practical examples from market-based flexibility provision, as well as referring to different stakeholders and their roles within the market. Challenges of flexibility markets which are discussed are vulnerability to participants' strategies, engaging a large number of flexibility resources, requirements for regulatory oversight, and the integration within existing sector organisation.

Keywords Flexibility market · Electricity distribution · Curtailment · Congestion management

6.1 Introduction

The net-zero emission aspiration in the energy sector and resulting energy transition has brought about three major technological shifts in distribution systems. Firstly, distributed and intermittent generation is increasing significantly. Secondly, energy consumption is becoming increasingly dispatchable, i.e., consumers are now more flexible to schedule their consumption. And lastly, electricity grids are implementing technologies which allow for controlling and optimising flows as well as relatively short-term adjustments in capacity. These features complement each other as intermittent generation requires that other aspects of the electricity system, such as demand and the grid capacity, adjust according to fluctuation in the supply. The potential of putting these new features into good use has given rise to extensive analysis and discussions as well as first implementations of markets and platforms to integrate and optimise flexibility on a local level.

The term flexibility is widely used and generally understood, yet difficult to define concisely. This is because it depends heavily on the context in which flexibility is needed and the from which it is provided. With regard to network users, flexibility is often coined as the ability and willingness to deviate upon request from a predefined baseline of generation or consumption (e.g., CEER, 2018) For an electric vehicle this baseline could be to charge in the evening after the owner comes back from work. The flexibility of a fleet of electric vehicles would then consist in shifting the recharging process, for example, into the night or even charging at an alternative location. Flexibility markets are referred to, for example, as a platform that makes flexibility demand and supply visible to each other (Radecke et al., 2019). Thus, the line can be blurry between evolving electricity markets and developing flexibility markets. Some types of electricity markets, such as nodal spot markets and intraday markets, cater for delivering or absorbing electricity at a certain point in time and specific physical location. Similarly, some flexibility services include the delivery or uptake of electricity and markets for such flexibility may resemble an intricate electricity market. In other settings, however, flexibility is traded as a service only, leaving those who provide it in charge of settling the related electricity trading in separate markets.

Flexibility can be supplied as up- or downward adjustment in the generation or load. Network users who inject electricity into the grid, provide positive flexibility by increasing their output. The same service is provided when network users who would normally withdraw electricity reduce their uptake. An additional dimension of flexibility is connected to control options. Some applications or use cases of flexibility may not even require an actual deviation from planned energy schedules. Instead, the mere readiness to adapt or respectively the ability to potentially control a schedule may constitute an instance of flexibility. This can be useful to some stakeholders in distribution systems and help with increasing the overall efficiency of the energy supply. An example for this would be a battery, which is available to withdraw and inject electricity as needed or requested. Alternatively, in a district heating system with other heat sources for backup, a heat pump can be made available for curtailment upon request. In the context of grid infrastructure flexibility can further refer to the possibility of accommodating additional flows with a relatively short notice. Network operators can achieve this with control equipment or grid enhancing technologies.

Historically, most of the present flexibility options in electricity systems were not available. At the same time, traditional electricity systems did not rely on flexibility nearly as much as today's innovative and sustainable electricity systems do. In a framework with large, central supply from relatively dispatchable thermal generators, flexibility was mostly needed for two purposes. On the one hand, it was (and in fact still is) required to buffer small forecasting errors for an otherwise fairly predictable and inelastic demand. Additionally, some flexibility was necessary as a backup to cover shortfall when there was an equipment failure. Thus, flexibility would buffer the effects of an unscheduled outage of a generation facility or of unanticipated demand change, for example, connected to unforeseen weather or unexpectedly popular media events. In such circumstances, thermal generators would ramp up or down to ensure that supply and demand match at all times. The network, on the other hand, was mostly designed with generous security margins to take up any expected electricity transfers.

This chapter provides an overview of benefits and potential problems in connection to trading flexibility services and their prospects to meet the challenges related to the electricity sector transition. In what follows, the chapter

- provides an overview of different design options for flexibility products and markets,

- discusses the challenges for flexibility markets in future distribution systems, and
- concludes on trading flexibility services in a decentralised manner.

6.2 Market and Product Design for Flexibility

The cost of flexibility generally reflects the opportunity cost of deviating from a set baseline or respectively of keeping ready to do so. If the compensation for a flexibility service exceeds the cost difference as compared to operating regularly, the flexibility provider gains from offering the service. The willingness to pay for a flexibility service, on the other hand, is defined by the cost of an alternative remedy for the needed flexibility. Thus, for example, when congestion can be relieved at a lower cost by paying a network user to reduce peak load than by expanding the grid, a flexibility market can help to match the network operator's demand with a suitable flexibility service from network users. In fact, European regulation, now requires distribution system operators of its member states to procure services in a market-based manner from distributed generation, demand response, or storage when they are cheaper than grid expansion (EU, 2019).

Flexibility services come in many different dimensions. The actual product design determines how flexibility would be employed and which assets can provide it. Product design in flexibility markets needs to balance the trade-off between dimensions that are specific to the types of assets providing flexibility, as well as to the purpose for which flexibility is procured. Relevant aspects include, for example, direction, duration, lead time, location, designated delivery time, reliability, control, ramping rate, and dispatch probability or predictability (Jin et al., 2020). Markets for flexibility services generally allocate flexibility in two different directions—i.e., positive and negative which mean adding electricity or capacity to the system or respectively reducing it. Postponing or replacing network expansion, for example, can intuitively be provided by consumers reducing their electricity demand or alternatively by a local generator providing additional electricity, thereby reducing the need to distribute electricity from the larger grid.

The duration and delivery time of flexibility provision is closely linked to certain use cases and supply contexts. Long-term contracts can be beneficial for network operators when seeking to replace network expansion. Additionally, with a long-term agreement flexibility providers have a reliable basis to invest into flexible assets. Short-term flexibility, on the other hand, harvests the potential of less predictable flexibility resources and supports system operation in case of temporary fluctuations. The advance time of contracting flexibility serves a similar purpose, with short advance contracts allowing for sourcing flexibility from less predictable network uses whereas long advances suiting the aim of deferring grid investment or enabling investments into flexible assets.

Some flexibility providers may be able to provide their flexibility service only at a specific time of the day or during a particular season. This is the case for example for electric vehicle fleets which usually operate during the day and charge at night or for hydro power plants for which the reservoirs regularly deplete during the summer. Especially, for long-term products, it is important to reflect these cycles to include this flexibility in the market. For example, in the piclo flexibility market in Great Britain, DSOs can purchase flexibility for longer periods which can be dispatched only during a prespecified service window within the contract period (cf. Schittekatte & Meeus, 2020).

Flexibility to relieve congestion is necessarily local. Services to balance a trading portfolio or for frequency control, on the other hand, are less location specific. Defining the specific location or grid area in which a network operator would demand flexibility to relieve congestion may not be trivial and the outcome may vary over time depending on the causes for congestion. Markets or platforms can group providers into different zones or locations, or assign for example a sensitivity or congestion relief factor indicating how well a specific provider alleviates a certain constraint, as it is the case for example in the enera flexibility market in Germany (cf. Radecke et al., 2019).

Some flexibility service can be provided in the form of a control option, meaning the flexibility provider agrees to a certain operating schedule or output band and deviates from it when called upon. For such flexibility products, the additional dimensions of ramping rate, dispatch probability, or predictability of dispatch are relevant. The contracted ramping rate should reflect, on the one hand, the technical abilities of assets that provide flexibility as well as the physical needs of the network operator and other flexibility demands. Very rapid ramping usually requires automated communication and control technology both on the side of the flexibility provider and for the party contracting the control option as well. For providers of control-based flexibility, it is furthermore important to assess or maybe even contractually settle the probability with which the flexibility is dispatched and to assess the predictability of being called to action. Generally, when the dispatch is predictable and occurs less frequently, it is cheaper for network users to provide flexibility.

The current discussion of flexibility markets and recent developments focus on network congestion. Network operators or system operators can use flexibility to resolve existing congestion (e.g., Jin et al., 2020; Radecke et al., 2019) and to replace or merely defer grid expansion. Linked to this, flexibility services can help network operators to address delays in delivering new capacity, provide voltage and frequency control, and other ancillary services (cf. Jin et al., 2020 for a more detailed overview). Additional demand for flexibility stems from balancing responsible parties who seek to compensate for imbalances. These can include retailers faced with fluctuations in supply or demand, or any party marketing fluctuating generation. While many mechanisms for the allocation are one-sided and cater to the network or system operator only, some markets accommodate other flexibility demands as well. Especially, where different demands for flexibility compete for the same resources, adequate market design is needed to ensure that the flexibility potential is utilised efficiently—i.e., the stakeholder that values it most receives the flexibility service first.

Various kinds of stakeholders participate in local flexibility markets. Larger generators or consumers may offer their flexibility directly. For smaller network users aggregators can act as intermediaries and help them handle market processes and prequalification. Aggregators can be independent parties that are specialised in aggregation or existing stakeholders such as retailers or balancing responsible parties. Also, flexibility market operation itself is a role that can either be independent or linked to different stakeholders (cf. Brandstätt et al., 2016). In many contexts, the network or system operator seems to be the intuitive option for market operation.

The market design for local flexibility services may differ in various aspects such as participation rules and prequalification, clearing or scoring and payments. Market rules relate closely, and have to align, with the types of products to be allocated, as discussed above. Firstly, participation of flexibility resources can be optional or alternatively be mandatorily linked to the participation in other relevant aspects of electricity supply. Participants in a system-wide wholesale market, for example, may be obliged to reverse their trades for redispatch in case of congestion. However, particularly, when network users participate voluntarily, the market operator may scrutinise potential participants in a prequalification process in order to ensure their technical ability, reliability, and financial stability. Thus, prequalification may merely require declaring information on the involved assets as well as on the service provider, but it may also include deposit payments and testing of the equipment. To ensure reliability, prequalification can be reassessed regularly and even revoked when a user has defaulted, or technical parameters have changed.

The selection and payment rules in a local flexibility market are closely related to the products traded. Remuneration can be per utilisation or dispatch, as well as cover a spread, per reserve capacity or refer to other features such as number of activations or a flat service fee (Anaya & Pollitt, 2020a). A flexibility market or platform may either collect bids in a tender over a certain period or clear them as soon as they match. Correspondingly, as in any other market the price can be pay-as-bid or as cleared—i.e., replicate the actual bids or represent the clearing margin. Some of the above features may be combined—i.e., tenders could be organised per constraint area for participation by providers that are prequalified in a predefined geographical area only, and several tenders for different types of services and periods may be held in parallel (Anaya & Pollitt, 2020b).

6.3 Challenges of Market-Based Flexibility Procurement

Some of the main challenges for procuring flexibility services in a market-based manner are

- incentivising participation of flexibility resources and investments in flexibility-enabling assets,
- integrating flexibility markets with other markets and allocation mechanisms,
- embedding flexibility markets into sector regulation, and
- ensuring coordination between grid operators and adjacent markets.

Standardisation of products plays an important role in motivating participation and new investments. Investments into new flexible assets depend on flexibility markets to ensure a revenue from flexibility. Product standardisation may simplify bidding and thus encourage flexibility providers to enter the market. However, the design of a flexibility product defines its suitability for a particular use case and consequently the willingness to pay. Trading a certain type of flexibility in a marketplace, and more importantly excluding others, can come down to picking winners. In addition to reduced participation and forgone investments, this may allocate the existing flexibility potential inefficiently. However, defining few and rather broad flexibility products increases the size of the market for a particular type of flexibility as compared to market segments for highly specialised flexibility services. Thus, flexibility markets with standardised products can benefit from higher liquidity not only due to larger market segments but also potentially due to market entry. Too simple and standardised flexibility products, however, may make it difficult to match supply and demand for specific dimensions. The calibration of standardised versus differentiated products ideally trades-off these contrary effects.

Furthermore, flexibility markets should blend in seamlessly with the existing architecture of electricity markets. If a flexibility service does not include the actual transfer of electricity, any party offering flexibility must align their electricity trading with the outcome of the flexibility market—i.e., electricity that has been sold in a regular market, for example day-ahead or intraday, must be offset in case a flexibility service requires downward regulation. To achieve this, the timelines of electricity and flexibility markets must be sufficiently aligned. In addition, local flexibility markets should ideally integrate well with existing mechanisms for balancing and redispatch. Many flexibility markets that have been implemented so far seek to add to rather than replace existing congestion management mechanisms (Radecke et al., 2019). Especially, when participation in other mechanisms is mandatory, friction between for example curtailment rules and flexibility provision may prevent flexibility providers from participating in the market. Furthermore, other mechanisms may affect the provision of flexibility. For example, load-based network charges (as discussed in Chapter 4) can hinder flexibility, if providers of upward flexibility services are faced with increased charges, when increasing feed-in or withdrawal load. Existing schemes of tariffs and levies often do not naturally enable local markets, yet changing the framework comes with significant distributional effects and may heavily distort incentives (e.g., Lüth et al., 2020). Additionally, flexibility markets need to blend in with existing network and balancing codes.

It is important that flexibility markets are carefully embedded into existing sector regulation. Firstly, network operators should have good incentives to procure flexibility services efficiently. Also, network operators' market activities need to be aligned with related investments into flexible equipment and grid expansion. Absent adequate regulation, network operators may prefer to expand the grid for any potential network use and benefit from capital expenditures instead of putting effort into managing congestion through cheaper ways. Even given sufficient incentives to prioritise flexibility over grid expansion, there remains some potential for discrimination when the system operator can influence the selection of flexibility providers. Particularly when network operation is integrated with other steps in the value chain, such as retail, generation, or storage, network operators can favour flexibility provision from their affiliated providers (for example via defining the specifications of flexibility resources they wish to purchase in the market in a way that are more favourable to their own resources). This is partially addressed when the market platform is operated by an independent operator and especially so, when all potential users have a say in decisions concerning the marketplace, such as with a common information platform (Brandstätt et al., 2016). Furthermore, there may be a need for oversight of the market with respect to the abuse of market power. Trading flexibility in too many dimensions may result in smaller market segments which may be vulnerable to strategic behaviour and market power. A distributed generator behind a constraint may be aware of its influence on the constraint and thus abuse market power when relieving this congestion or even intentionally worsen it to profit from congestion relief (cf. Hirth & Schlecht, 2019). However, the preconditions for this strategy to be successful may be quite stringent and seemingly this challenge can be addressed by adequate market design and regulatory oversight (e.g., Cramton, 2019; Palovic et al., 2021).

Lastly, a commonly discussed challenge is coordination between different flexibility markets. This concerns the coordination of demands for flexibility from different network operators as well as procurements and trades in other markets. Depending on the details of sector organisation in a particular jurisdiction, the responsibility for reliability and grid adequacy may fall with the operator of the transmission or distribution system or both. Consequently, the demand for flexibility can come from either one or even both of them at the same time. However, even if for example, the procurement of flexibility is performed solely and entirely by the transmission operator, operation at the distribution level might still be affected as most flexibility providers are located there. This intensifies the need for coordination between grid operators at transmission and distribution levels (Schittekatte & Meus, 2020; Villar et al., 2018).

Furthermore, since flexibility markets are often local, it is likely that there would be several adjacent markets, unless consolidations happen due to regulation or competition. Given varying types of providers and the innovative forces of competition a setup with several neighbouring markets might well be efficient. However, the interoperability of adjacent markets is desirable, particularly if they are to be used efficiently by overarching network operators.

6.4 Conclusion

In distribution systems with increasing congestion and new active and flexible users, local markets for flexibility service gain importance and become increasingly widespread. They can be one-sided markets catering to the congestion management needs of a network operator or multi-sided platforms which also satisfy other flexibility demands for example by retailers or balancing responsible parties. Correspondingly, to those varying purposes of such markets, the spectrum for product and market design is wide.

Product design spans different physical dimensions, such as time and location, as well as control options and optionality. The design of local flexibility markets may differ, for example, regarding participation rules and prequalification and with respect to clearing or scoring as well as payments. Both product and market design need to suit flexibility providers as well as cover dimensions in which flexibility is demanded.

In addition to allocating existing flexibility efficiently, markets seek to include a large amount of flexibility resources and potentially even motivate additional investments. Key challenges are the integration of flexibility markets with other electricity markets and existing regulation as well as designing suitable allocation mechanisms. Also, local flexibility markets raise the challenge of coordinating the flexibility needs and flexibility provision between different voltage levels and adjacent grids or market areas.

Several pioneering markets are facilitated via government regulation or receiving some kind of support as demonstration projects. The growth of these markets will likely entail changes in the sector, for example, concerning network or retail tariffs and may require additional regulation with regard to smart technology and new roles within the electricity sector. In addition to product and market design for the efficient allocation of flexibility, we expect further discussions and research, for example, on the impact of flexibility markets on supply security given the electricity system transition towards the net-zero-carbon emission target.

References

Anaya, K. L., & Pollitt, M. G. (2020a). *Regulation and policies for local flexibility markets: Current and future developments in seven leading countries* (Report on MERLIN-Milestone 3). Energy Policy Research Group, University of Cambridge.

Anaya, K. L., & Pollitt, M. G. (2020b). *A review of international experience in the use of smart electricity platforms for the procurement of flexibility services* (Report on MERLIN-Milestone 2, part 2). Energy Policy Research Group, University of Cambridge.

Brandstätt, C., Brunekreeft, G., Buchmann, M., & Friedrichsen, N. (2016). Balancing between competition and coordination in smart grids—A Common Information Platform (CIP). *Economics of Energy & Environmental Policy, 6*(1), 93–109.

CEER. (2018). *Flexibility use at distribution level* (CEER Conclusions Paper, C18-DS-42-04).

Cramton, P. (2019). *Local flexibility market* (Working paper).

EU, European Union. (2019). Directive 2019/944 of the European Parliament and of the Council on Common Rules for the Internal Market for Electricity and Amending Directive 2012/27/EU.

Hirth, L., & Schlecht, I. (2019). *Redispatch Markets in Zonal Electricity Markets: Inc-Dec Gaming as a Consequence of Inconsistent Power Market Design (not Market Power)* (Working Paper). ZBW—Leibniz Information Centre for Economics.

Jin, X., Wu, Q., & Jia, H. (2020). Local flexibility markets: Literature review on concepts, models and clearing methods. *Applied Energy, 261*, 114387.

Lüth, A., Weibezahn, J., & Zepter, J. M. (2020). On Distributional effects in local electricity market designs—Evidence from a German case study. *Energies, 13*(8), 1993.

Palovic, M., Brandstätt, C., Buchmann, M., & Brunekreeft, G. (2021). *Strategisches Verhalten bei marktbasiertem Redispatch: Die internationalen Erfahrungen* (Bremen Energy Working Papers No. 36). Jacobs University Bremen.

Radecke, J., Hefele, J., & Hirth, L. (2019). *Markets for local flexibility in distribution networks* (Working Paper). ZBW—Leibniz Information Centre for Economics.

Schittekatte, T., & Meeus, L. (2020). Flexibility markets: Q&A with project pioneers. *Utilities Policy, 63*, 101017.

Villar, J., Bessa, R., & Matos, M. (2018). Flexibility products and markets: Literature review. *Electronic Power Systems Research, 154*, 329–340.

CHAPTER 7

Electricity Distribution Networks in the Context of Energy System Integration

Abstract This chapter examines how the decentralised energy paradigm fits within the context of the broader energy system transition. The shift towards more distributed forms of electricity provision is taking place in the context of broader energy system trends including the electrification of mobility and transport, smart and efficient energy management of buildings and the decarbonisation of heating and cooling. We frame decentralisation in the context of broader energy system integration by examining multi-energy systems and analysing the interactions across five system perspectives—fuel, spatial, temporal, service, and network. On this basis the energy system at the distribution is likely to be become increasingly interconnected and a proactive approach to coordination is likely to best position the system to manage risks and exploit opportunities.

Keywords Energy system integration · Distributed energy coordination · Multi-energy systems · Integrated energy systems

7.1 Introduction

In order to mitigate the worst effects of anthropogenic climate change, economies around the world will need to reduce dangerous greenhouse gas emissions. This has driven many major economies around the world to set ambitious net-zero objectives. In the near-term, the decarbonisation of the electricity sector has been proposed as the most achievable initiative to set economies along the pathway towards net zero. As described throughout the chapters of this book, the decentralisation of the electricity sector and the proliferation of distributed energy resources (DER) present as critical components of the electricity system transition pathways towards net zero, via the adoption of current technologies such as rooftop solar and distributed storage. However, the large-scale decarbonisation of sectors such as mobility, buildings, and heat are also critical for the mitigation of climate change effects. In this vein, net-zero pathways rely, in large part, upon the large-scale electrification of currently fossil-dominated energy vectors, especially for mobility and heating, combined with a shift towards alternative fuel sources such as hydrogen and biomass. Yet there are decentralisation and distributed resource imperatives across all of these vectors.

Traditional model of operations and planning tend to decouple between energy sector vectors including most apparently the sectional split between electricity market operation and gas market operation. This has taken place despite there always being close interactions between the vectors. Over time, however focus has been increasingly given to interlinkages and interactions between the vectors, and to considerations of how the planning and operation of such vectors could benefit from recognition and incorporation of such interlinkages. Initially, these linkages were approached from specific perspectives focussing for example on particular linkages between vectors—such as between the electricity and natural gas vectors (under the concept of electricity-gas co-optimisation) or combined heat-and-power (Chicco & Mancarella, 2009). More recently however it has been recognised that there is a need for a focus on the concept of the integration of energy systems itself.

There are a variety of challenges and opportunities in integrating distributed multi-energy systems, particularly under the increasingly rapid transition timeline required for successful climate change mitigation. Thus this chapter assesses the integration of energy systems in a distributed context and highlights the benefits of co-planning and co-operation approaches. The concept of multi-energy systems is a helpful conceptual approach to frame interactions that are expected to occur at the distribution level and issues associated with managing a smooth transition under high distributed resource penetrations. In Sect. 7.2 we introduce the concept of multi-energy systems as it relates to distributed systems and assess interactions at a multiplicity of different levels namely: (i) fuel interactions, (ii) service interactions, (iii) spatial interactions, (iv) temporal interactions, and (v) network interactions and highlight the interactions of most interest in managing transition. Finally, in Sect. 7.3, we conclude with policy implications and argue for a need to more closely coordinate planning, operations, and governance of distributed multi-energy systems.

7.2 Multi-energy Distributed Systems

The discipline of *multi-energy systems* has emerged to provide an assessment framework for the interactions between energy systems at various levels. Multi-energy systems consider a whole system approach to optimisation and evaluation of specific cases under study and an explicit expansion of system boundaries beyond subsectors (Guelpa et al., 2019; Mancarella, 2014). The strategic objective of multi-energy systems research is the development of consistent and appropriate approaches for the design, planning, modelling, and operation of unified energy systems to make the infrastructures increasingly flexible (Guelpa et al., 2019).

While multi-energy systems can be applied at a variety of scales, they have had particular application to smaller-scale resources within the distribution system (G Strauss et al., 2008). As it relates to the energy system transition and decarbonisation, two areas are particularly important in a distributed context. First, the decarbonisation of mobility and transport is intricately associated with distributed systems, particularly given the focus on large-scale electrification of passenger and commercial vehicles as a critical pathway. While light duty vehicles (LDV) are currently the largest total emitter of CO_2 of all transport modes they are expected by 2040 to be one of the smallest transport mode emitters (IEA, 2021). Given their scale, LDVs are intricately connected with energy consumers at the distribution level. Second, buildings are also critical in the analysis of energy system interactions at the distribution level. The decarbonisation of buildings are expected to play an important role in energy system decarbonisation. Residential buildings make up for around 27% of global final energy consumption and around 17% of global carbon emissions (Nejat et al., 2015). Moreover, demand for heating and cooling continues to grow especially in developing markets in line with growing energy access and income (Leibowicz et al., 2018). As such the decarbonisation of buildings especially at residential and smaller commercial scales continues to make up an important pathway on the 1.5 degree warming roadmap (IPCC, 2018, 2021). Both are expected to have particular application in multi-energy systems given the potential for whole-of-system optimisation at the distribution level.

In analysing interactions in the distribution system, there are five perspectives that are relevant. Mancarella (2014) sets out four of them being (i) spatial interactions, (ii) network interactions, (iii) fuel interactions, and (iv) service interactions. Additionally the temporal perspective is also relevant—with an understanding of how resources can be better coordinated across different times of the day or seasons as well.

Spatial interactions focus upon different levels of aggregation and sizing of distributed resources. At the smallest level this applies to individual buildings to district or local community aggregations, to regional or even national aggregations (Mancarella, 2014). The building setting presents opportunities for home and building owners to efficiently and dynamically manage energy requirements on a coordinated basis, co-optimising between their own needs, cost management and tariffs, and the opportunities available from trading energy use and flexibility in local distributed and wholesale markets (Shao et al., 2019). This level benefits from relatively unfettered energy control and specification of preferences from smaller groups of individuals or businesses (i.e., individuals within a household, or lessees within a building). This presents opportunities for DER flexibility enabled by coordinated and automated control of heating and cooling; appliances and equipment; and charging and discharging of electric vehicles. As the sizing moves from an individual premise to groups of premises, control of multiple units becomes more complex, emphasising the importance of alternative coordination methods and smart control algorithms that effectively manage the preservation of quality of service and optimisation of the aggregated fleet. At even larger levels of spatial aggregation (large local, regional, or system), direct control gives way to mechanisms for indirect and implicit coordination, with the need to manage imbalances in service response. From a locational perspective this also presents the opportunity to harnessing the heterogenous characteristics of resources located in different areas, but within the same spatial coordination boundary (Good et al., 2017). Consider for example, the ability to coordinate solar resources with differential clouding conditions across a region or optimising between different wind patterns in regional areas.

Fuel interactions examine the potential for integration of inputs for both electrical and thermal energy. Classical interactions between fossil sources have shifted towards analyses incorporating renewable or low-carbon sources such as wind and solar, geothermal, biomass/biofuels, and waste-to-energy (Mancarella, 2014). Also of interest in this energy transition era, is the management of interactions between conventional fossil fuels and renewables. In the management of energy balance at the distribution level, a critical interaction is the management of portfolios of intermittent or as-available resources—taking advantage of generation availability diversity such as between wind and solar and small-scale hydro, to higher availability sources (such as liquid or gaseous fuels, and geothermal resources). An added dimension in recent years is the potential for distributed storage (both stationary or vehicle-to-grid resources) to complement solar and wind DER portfolios. This becomes increasingly important given the ability this provides to actively manage the emissions profile of distributed systems, in the face of a need to rapidly decarbonise the electricity system.

Service interactions relate to the coordination of various outputs that distributed resources or multi-energy system can produce. This can be examined from the perspective of end-use energy vectors such as the delivery of electricity, heating and cooling services. These services can be delivered onsite for self-consumption but also for community, regional, or system consumption through networks (such as electricity and gas distribution, but also district energy for heating and cooling). Moreover interactions are also important to manage with respect to delivery of more granular services that apply within an energy vector. Most relevantly for the electricity system, DER offers the potential to provide not only energy but a range of system services including regulation, response, and reserves to manage system parameters including frequency and voltage (Eid et al., 2016). The flexible capabilities of DER can be harnessed also to provide multiple services at one time. This requires market and institutional frameworks that enable distributed multi-energy system participation through the removal of barriers to entry. Capacity and service specification restrictions have been of particular relevance—especially in relation to removing existing size barriers, and carefully adapting service specifications that enable new technologies (such as advanced inverters) without compromising system security.

Energy networks play a critical role in providing the interconnection between distributed resources to enable better coordination and integration between them. This has related to transmission and distribution networks to enable the dynamic transfer and flow of electricity and gas around systems, but also needs now to be expanded to considerations of electro-mobility networks (such as EV charging infrastructure networks). In order for energy networks to play the role as a facilitator of DER, traditional approaches to the operational management of networks need to adapt from more passive network (which have traditionally focused upon network monitoring, reactive reconfiguration, and maintenance) roles to more active operational management. This could involve for example through active generation and load dispatch, dynamic control of network resources (including storage and flexible alternating current transmission system (FACTS)) and the specification, procurement, and dispatch of a wider range of system services. This aligns with the transition of operational roles from a distribution network operator to a distribution system operator and platform provider (Chapter 3).

Finally, temporal considerations also require consideration. This relates to the management of distributed energy resources across different time periods. This could be over shorter periods, such as a day or week (with a famous example being the duck-curve effect observed in DER rich regions), to medium-term periods, such as intra-annual seasonal energy management, to longer term inter-annual periods—such as consideration of multi-year weather patterns (e.g., El Nino, La Nina, etc.). In the shorter term, this becomes a focus of the system operator, but over the longer term system planning for integration becomes ever more important.

7.3 Policy Implications and Conclusions

Under the lens of multi-energy systems, distributed energy resources introduce a multitude of integration considerations relevant to the planning and operation of an energy distribution network. Moreover, interactions arise at multiple levels and integration issues need be considered from a variety of perspectives. At low levels of DER penetration many of these issues may well be hidden but as DER penetration grows, these integration issues are likely to become more apparent.

At a policy level, a number of regulatory barriers exist to the integration of energy systems. These include the cost and risk of integrating technologies, institutional constraints to encouraging innovation, limited coordination between grid operators (i.e., between the transmission system operator and the distribution system operator), access to data, consumer acceptance, and behaviour of prosumers themselves (Cambini et al., 2020).

This suggests a need for a deliberate and proactive approach at the policy level that caters to the interaction between multiple energy systems (Jamasb & Llorca, 2018) including the need to continuously evaluate the system to assess its greatest possible coordination potential (O'malley et al., 2016).

Among the measures highlighted as important for facilitating better integration include (i) specific incentives for encouraging innovation—including network level total expenditure incentives and through the implementation of regulatory sandboxes (Cambini et al., 2020), tariff reform including connection and use-of-system charges (Cossent et al., 2009) and incentives for active consumer engagement and the entry of new market players. Creating specific objectives for TSO/DSO coordination is also important including the potential for asset ownership and operation (Ugarte et al., 2015) and the potential for an integrated Energy System Operator that co-optimises 'electrons and molecules' (Nillesen et al., 2020). While the range of measures should be adapted to suit the specific characteristics and topology of the system under consideration it is apparent, given the potential for increasing complexity flowing from multi-energy distributed systems, that local and distributed energy markets and systems should be designed with integration at front-of-mind.

References

Cambini, C., Congiu, R., Jamasb, T., Llorca, M., & Soroush, G. (2020). Energy systems integration: Implications for public policy. *Energy Policy, 143.* https://doi.org/10.1016/J.ENPOL.2020.111609

Chicco, G., & Mancarella, P. (2009). Distributed multi-generation: A comprehensive view. *Renewable and Sustainable Energy Reviews, 13*(3), 535–551. https://doi.org/10.1016/J.RSER.2007.11.014

Cossent, R., Gómez, T., & Frías, P. (2009). Towards a future with large penetration of distributed generation: Is the current regulation of electricity distribution ready? Regulatory recommendations under a European perspective. *Energy Policy, 37*(3), 1145–1155. https://doi.org/10.1016/J.ENPOL.2008.11.011

Eid, C., Codani, P., Perez, Y., Reneses, J., & Hakvoort, R. (2016). Managing electric flexibility from distributed energy resources: A review of incentives for market design. *Renewable and Sustainable Energy Reviews, 64,* 237–247. https://doi.org/10.1016/J.RSER.2016.06.008

G Strauss, P. C., Braun, M., & Strauss, P. (2008). A review on aggregation approaches of controllable distributed energy units in electrical power systems. *Strauss International Journal of Distributed Energy Resources, 4*(4), 17. http://www.ts-publishers.com

Good, N., Martínez Ceseña, E. A., & Mancarella, P. (2017). Ten questions concerning smart districts. *Building and Environment, 118,* 362–376. https://doi.org/10.1016/J.BUILDENV.2017.03.037

Guelpa, E., Bischi, A., Verda, V., Chertkov, M., & Lund, H. (2019). Towards future infrastructures for sustainable multi-energy systems: A review. *Energy, 184,* 2–21. https://doi.org/10.1016/J.ENERGY.2019.05.057

IEA. (2021). *Net zero by 2050—A roadmap for the global energy sector.* https://iea.blob.core.windows.net/assets/beceb956-0dcf-4d73-89fe-1310e3046d68/NetZeroby2050-ARoadmapfortheGlobalEnergySector_CORR.pdf

IPCC. (2018). *IPCC special report: Global warming of 1.5°C.* https://doi.org/10.1016/j.oneear.2019.10.025

IPCC. (2021). *Sixth assessment report, climate change 2021: The physical science basis.* https://www.ipcc.ch/assessment-report/ar6/

Jamasb, T., & Llorca, M. (2018). *Energy systems integration: Economics of a new paradigm.* www.eprg.group.cam.ac.uk

Leibowicz, B. D., Lanham, C. M., Brozynski, M. T., Vázquez-Canteli, J. R., Castejón, N. C., & Nagy, Z. (2018). Optimal decarbonization pathways for urban residential building energy services. *Applied Energy, 230,* 1311–1325. https://doi.org/10.1016/J.APENERGY.2018.09.046

Mancarella, P. (2014). MES (multi-energy systems): An overview of concepts and evaluation models. *Energy, 65,* 1–17. https://doi.org/10.1016/j.energy.2013.10.041

Nejat, P., Jomehzadeh, F., Taheri, M. M., Gohari, M., & Muhd, M. Z. (2015). A global review of energy consumption, CO2 emissions and policy in the residential sector (with an overview of the top ten CO2 emitting countries). *Renewable and Sustainable Energy Reviews, 43,* 843–862. https://doi.org/10.1016/J.RSER.2014.11.066

Nillesen, P., van Nunen, R., & Witzemann, M. (2020). Hydrogen and the emergence of the energy system operator. *OIES Energy Forum, 124,* 49–54.

O'malley, M., Kroposki, B., Hannegan, B., Madsen, H., Andersson, M., D'haeseleer, W., Mcgranaghan, M. F., Dent, C., Strbac, G., Baskaran, S., & Rinker,

M. (2016). *The joint institute for strategic energy systems integration: Defining and describing the value proposition.* https://doi.org/10.2172/1257674

Shao, C., Ding, Y., Siano, P., & Lin, Z. (2019). A framework for incorporating demand response of smart buildings into the integrated heat and electricity energy system. *IEEE Transactions on Industrial Electronics, 66*(2), 1465–1475. https://doi.org/10.1109/TIE.2017.2784393

Ugarte, S., Larkin, J., Ree, B. Van der, Swinkels, V., Voog, M., Friedichsen, N., Michaels, J., Thielmann, A., Wietschel, M., & Villafafila, R. (2015). *Energy storage: Which market designs and regulatory incentives are needed?*

CHAPTER 8

Unbundling in Electricity Distribution Networks

Abstract The liberalisation of the electricity sector has resulted in structural changes to the industry, one of the most important of which was the separation of network-related businesses from competitive functions such as generation and retail supply. The main motivation for unbundling of electricity supply chain was to encourage competition, prevent cross subsidies between regulated and non-regulated activities, and encourage focused managerial effort among network companies to improve their cost efficiency and their quality of network service. Although these points are well established for transmission networks, the issue at the distribution network level is not straightforward due to its complexity. Thus, unbundling of distribution networks can take a different path although useful lessons can be drawn from experiences at the bulk power system.

Keywords Ownership unbundling · Legal unbundling · Independent system operator · Competition and coordination

© The Author(s), under exclusive license to Springer Nature Switzerland AG 2022
R. Poudineh et al., *Electricity Distribution Networks in the Decentralisation Era*,
https://doi.org/10.1007/978-3-030-98069-6_8

8.1 Introduction

The bulk power system has traditionally been the focus of the electricity sector restructuring debate. This had made sense in the past as nearly all generation facilities were connected to the transmission network thus there was a significant opportunity for efficiency gain in this segment through competition and incentive alignment for transmission grid ownership and system operation. However, with the growth of distributed energy resources (DERs) such as solar PV, battery, EVs, flexible demand, etc., the restructuring debate has extended all the way down to low-voltage distribution networks.

At the transmission grid level, restructuring involves unbundling of network segment, which is a natural monopoly, from generation business which is potentially competitive. In the European Union (EU) region a strong drive for liberalisation was started since the end of last century with the aim of brining competition to the electricity and gas sectors, lowering energy prices and maximising the benefit to end users. Similar initiates were also implemented in other countries such as Chile, Argentina, and the US. Initially, regulators in the EU and the US were of the view that functional and legal unbundling are sufficient measures to promote competition and provide non-discriminatory access to the grid. However, it later turned out that without structural separation of network from generation, there is a risk of discriminatory behaviour by integrated utilities in terms of access to the network and commercially relevant information as well as investment in the network.[1]

In the EU region, the regulation on unbundling has been changing over time and becoming more stringent. The default option envisioned for gas and electricity transmission is ownership unbundling according to Third Energy Package adopted in 2009. However, the Third Energy package does not require ownership unbundling for distribution networks and also it exempts networks with less than 100,000 customers from unbundling requirements. The updated Clean Energy Package of 2019

---

[1] A firm that controls the electricity network and is involved also in the competitive parts of the value chain has an obvious interest to restrict or deny grid access to other firms that are active in the upstream or downstream of supply chain. Therefore, ensuring a just, transparent, and non-discriminatory access to network capacity for all market participants is a precondition to achieve optimum competition in the sector. Introducing structural unbundling removes not only the possibility of discriminatory behaviour by the network owner/operator but also eases the process of regulatory oversight.

has not changed these regulations but has allowed for the possibility that network operators own/operate storage facilities and EV charging points.

Although there are useful insights from the bulk power system for unbundling at the low-voltage distribution network, there are fundamentally different issues at the distribution grid level which makes the direct application of bulk power system rules to this segment ineffective (Pérez-Arriaga et al., 2016). First, due to a high number of components, distribution networks are more complex compared with transmission systems. This not only increases the regulatory burden to determine the efficient cost of these utilities but also makes it less beneficial to decouple network planning from operation because of the loss of economy of scope. Second, as opposed to the transmission system, markets for distribution system services are local and less liquid. This means that higher degrees of market monitoring are required to prevent exercise of market power. Third, in the transmission system, energy loss and network constraints are often reflected in the prices in the form of nodal pricing or zonal pricing (as an approximation of nodal pricing). However, users connected to distribution networks receive a regulated price signal which is usually embedded in retail tariffs. Such regulated tariffs do not convey information about the cost and value of energy at specific times and locations within the network. In the absence of efficient pricing, distribution networks are likely to face higher levels of congestions especially in regions with higher penetrations of DERs. This all means that restructuring at the distribution network level can take a different form that does not necessarily coincide with that of the transmission system.

This chapter analyses the issue of electricity distribution system unbundling. The next section discusses the economics of unbundling and explores various options available to arrange the structure of the electricity distribution sector. Section 8.3 investigates the implications of distribution sector unbundling models for the growth of DERs, retail market competition, and network service quality. Section 8.4 examines the issue of information and data management at the distribution sector level. Finally, Sect. 8.5 provides the concluding remarks.

8.2 Economics of Unbundling

Similar to rail transport and telecommunication, the electricity sector is a network-based industry. This has implications for industry structure, governance model and competition. Electricity networks (both transmission and distribution) are natural monopiles. A natural monopoly makes provision of network service by a single company more efficient compared with two or more. This is because the costs of these companies are such that the capital cost dominates thus average cost declines fast as the output increases. This in turn creates high economies of scale and consequently barrier to new entry. As a result, the network segment of electricity supply chain has been subject to economic regulation to prevent the abuse of monopoly position.

Unlike the network segment, generation and retails are potentially competitive. This is why, following the liberalisation of the electricity sector in 1990s, the network segment was unbundled from generation and retail supply.[2] Key benefits stated in the literature for unbundling are that it can stimulate competition and increase efficiency, simplify the market structure, enable privatisation, and improve the security of supply (Baarsma et al., 2007).

When networks are unbundled from generation and retail, the internal coordination that previously happened in the integrated utility now must be achieved through a combination of market mechanism (e.g., contracts) and regulated charges. Thus, unbundling needs to be combined with the design of efficient coordination mechanisms (network tariffs, contractual arrangements, side-payments, etc.) (Brunekreeft, 2015). However, the implementation of efficient network charging regime is not straightforward because of issues such as regulatory restrictions, transactions and regulatory costs, lack of information, etc. Overall unbundling can also have some disadvantages too such as preventing coordination, causing direct cost, reducing synergy, and increasing transaction costs (Baarsma et al., 2007). Despite this, when the reform of electricity sector is carried out properly, the empirical evidence shows that it generally improves the efficiency of the sector (Jamasb et al., 2017).

Unbundling can take various forms ranging from accounting and legal (weaker) separation to ownership (stronger) unbundling. The accounting unbundling requires the integrated utility to keep separate accounts for the network business versus commercially competitive activities such as generation and supply. Legal unbundling means to have separate legal entities in charge of the network business and competitive activities although they might still belong to the same firm. Ownership

---

[2] In some places, such as the US, it was only the transmission grid that was unbundled whereas in other places such as the UK both transmission and distribution networks were unbundled.

unbundling, on the other hand, is the strongest form of unbundling which requires having completely sperate owners for the network versus generation and supply. This form of unbundling removes the potential for discriminatory behaviour and is more conductive to a competitive market.

The choice about the form of unbundling depends on various factors such as wider sector policies, historical development of the electricity sector, political and economic contexts, and the degree of resistance by incumbent integrated utility, among others. Weaker forms of unbundling are easier to implement both from a procedure perspective and politically however they might not completely remove misalignment of incentives between the integrated utility and independent generation plants. The stronger forms of unbundling are less straightforward to implement but they better promote competition.

8.2.1 Unbundling Options for Distribution Networks

At the transmission level, legal or administrative unbundling is often the first step after moving away from the vertically integrated utility company. The preferred model by regulators especially in Europe and the US however is ownership unbundling in which the network ownership and operation (TSO) and generation businesses (GENCO) are undertaken by completely different companies. In some jurisdictions there is also a preference for an independent system operator (ISO) which basically separates the owner of network (TO) from the system operator. This later model removes the disincentivise of the network owner to adopt non-network solutions as such initiatives often entail less regulatory assets and consequently less revenue for the network owner. Figure 8.1 presents the spectrum of models available for the governance of the electricity transmission system.

Similar to the transmission system, various options have been proposed for restructuring of the electricity distribution sector. All these models focus on allocating the responsibility of key functions of the sector (i.e., market operation, system operation, and network ownership/operation) to one or more entities. The experience of bulk power system provides useful insights here but as mentioned previously, given the different nature of issues at the distribution level the optimum solution is not as straightforward as the transmission system.

Pérez-Arriaga et al. (2016) analyse three options for the structure of the distribution sector (Fig. 8.2). The first option is a Distribu-

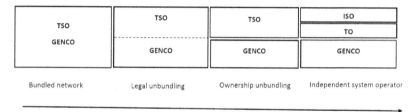

Fig. 8.1 The spectrum of unbundling models in the electricity transmission network (*Source* authors)

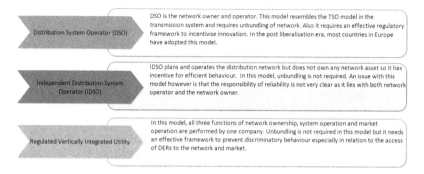

Fig. 8.2 Three options for the structure of the electricity distribution sector (*Source* authors)

tion System Operator (DSO) which basically mimics the TSO model in the transmission system. In this model, DSO is the network owner and responsible for investment in and operation of the distribution grid including active network management through running markets for procurement of network services within its service area (such as voltage support and reactive power). This model requires ownership separation of DSO from generation and retail supply. It also requires an effective regulatory framework to incentivise innovation especially for integration of DERs and adoption of digital technologies. In the post-liberalisation era, most countries in Europe have adopted this model.

The second option is to have an independent distribution system operator (IDSO) like ISO at the transmission level. The IDSO plans and operates the distribution network but does not own any network asset. This incentivises IDSO to manage distribution network in an active and efficient manner through considering both network and non-network solutions. The responsibility of investment in the network is with the network owner based on suggestions by IDSO and regulatory approval (although IDSO cannot force any particular investment plan on the networks owner and the owner has some degree of autonomy over the way which investments are carried out). In this model, the distribution network owner does not need to become unbundled from generation and retail supply. An issue with this model however is that the responsibility of reliability is not very clear as it lies with both IDSO and the network owner and not solely with either one, something which may result in free rider problems (Burger et al., 2019).

The third model is a closely regulated vertically integrated utility. In this model, all three functions of network ownership, system operation, and market platform are incorporated into one company. The distribution company can also engage in the generation business as well as the retail supply. The key issue with this model is application of an effective framework to prevent discriminatory behaviour by the monopoly company especially in relation to the access of DERs to the network and market. Design and implementation of such regulations however are not straightforward in practice.

It is also possible to have a variation of these models. For example, an independent market operator for the distribution sector can be established which operates a market for flexibility services over a larger area than the service area of a single distribution network. There is also possibility of combining the role of ISO and IDSO especially for the meshed part of the distribution network at sub-transmission level. Nonetheless, there are several arguments against separation of the role of distribution system operation (IDSO) from the distribution network operator/owner (DNO) (Burger et al., 2019). First is that the coordination between DNO and IDSO can be challenging as it needs to rely on a complex contractual mechanism. The second issue is that the cost and complexity of the separation may be more than any future benefit that such a separation provides. Finally, the third issue is, with the growth of DERs the need for information sharing between DNO and IDSO, at various time scales, increases significantly. Therefore, if there is no efficient protocol of communication, there is a higher risk of service disruption and increased costs to end users.

From an economic perspective, a key point to consider when choosing the governance model for the distribution sector is the trade-off between coordination and competition at this segment of supply chain. The separation of system operation from the network ownership at the distribution level is likely to result in more transaction costs than any competition benefit that it can provide. The coordination between system operator and network owner needs to happen either through a market-based mechanism or bilateral contracts. Because of complexity of the system and specificity of the asset in terms of use, timing, and location, bilateral contracts have been argued to be a more effective approach compared with the market-based coordination in this context (Burger et al., 2019). However, negotiating a complete contract for installation and maintenance of millions of distribution network assets is likely to face a high transaction cost compared with the model in which the network owner (DNO) and the system operator are integrated. Also, many of the DNOs are small and benefits of separation of the system operation and network ownership for them may not justify the regulatory burden and cost of decoupling.

The growth of decentralisation paradigm and the emergence of distributed energy resources (DERs) have resulted in a debate about whether DNOs should be allowed to own and operate DERs, or such activities should be left to competitive providers. This is specifically important as DERs not only impact the operation of distribution networks but sometimes are more efficient alternatives to traditional network investments. The same question also applies to the retail market given that the demand aggregation shares many of the characteristics of DERs aggregation. In the next subsection we discuss these issues.

8.3 Unbundling Effect on the Growth of DERs, Retail Market Competition, and Network Service Quality

Deployment of DERs is a competitive business thus it is natural to assume that such activities need to be outside the scope of distribution network companies' operation. Despite that, some regulatory authorities (such as in New York) have allowed distribution network companies to own and operate DERs if they can demonstrate that such projects meet certain conditions such as: they cannot be efficiently and/or adequately provided by competitive providers, they provide system benefits and are cheaper than traditional network investment, or the project is for demonstration purposes (Burger et al., 2019). There are also arguments that due to specificity of capital, timing, and location of DERs deployment, network companies are better positioned to provide them than market participants (Brunekreeft & Ehlers, 2006). Furthermore, it is also argued that network companies incur lower capital costs compared with competitive providers thus they can provide DERs cheaper.

However, there are a set of important issues that need to be considered if DERs are included within the scope of operation of distribution networks (Burger et al., 2019). First, distribution network ownership of DERs can lead to underutilisation of these assets in places where unbundling rules exist. This is because when DERs are classified as network assets, they are often only allowed to provide services to the network and cannot obtain additional revenues by participating in the competitive market. Second, due to information asymmetry, regulator would not be able to effectively monitor the cost and usefulness of deployment of DERs by network companies. This would likely result in higher costs of procurement compared with the case that distributed energy resources are installed by competitive providers. Third, independent competitive providers are likely to provide the same set of services as an integrated distribution network company, cost efficiently. Finally, the low cost of capital of network companies is not necessarily due to their efficiency but because of the nature of their regulated assets that transfer the risks to rate payers.

Therefore, considering all the advantages and disadvantages of monopolistic provision of DERs, it seems the arguments weigh in favour of competitive provision of these services. Effective regulation can be a proxy for vertical integration by network companies. Poudineh and Jamasb (2014) propose a contractual arrangement that allows distribution companies to procure the service of distributed generation, storage, demand response, and energy efficiency as alternative to grid capacity enhancement. The assumption here is that distribution network companies are incentivised through economic regulation to consider non-wire investments where such solutions are more efficient compared with traditional network investment. It also implies moving away from the traditional model of passive distribution network management through overengineering to active network management.

Several countries now are providing these types of incentives for network companies. In the EU, regulation exists that encourages distribution networks to procure the services of distributed resources. In the UK, Ofgem has been incentivising adoption of innovative non-network solutions which can avoid or defer the need for grid investment through the RIIO regulatory framework.[3] It is expected that more countries consider such incentives in their regulatory framework of distribution network companies.[4]

Another issue of interest is how unbundling might affect retail competition and service quality. There is a wide consensus that unbundling (especially the legal form) improves retail competition and promotes lower prices. It is also expected to improve network service quality because of the more managerial focus, increased investment, and improvement in the regulatory effectiveness (Nillesen & Pollitt, 2019). However, as discussed previously, there are various forms of unbundling. While legal unbundling is considered to have positive effects there are disagreements on the implications of strongest form of unbundling (i.e., ownership unbundling) especially when they are forced upon distribution utilities.

The Nillesen and Pollitt (2019) review of both theoretical and empirical papers shows that evidence is either not in favour of ownership unbundling of distribution networks or is inconclusive about it. This is even more pronounced when the cost dimension is examined as most studies surveyed conclude that ownership unbundling has a negative impact on the cost of network operation. The authors also review the experience of the Netherlands and New Zealand and conclude that there

---

[3] One of the key aspects of the RIIO framework is the total expenditure approach (totex). This approach combines a portion of utility capital expenditures (capex) and operating expenditures (opex) into one regulatory asset that allows a rate of return on both, based on a predefined percentage split. This eliminates the incentive for over capitalisation and excessive investment in hard assets such as wires and transformers. Instead, it encourages distribution utilities to seek the most cost-effective solution for network issues. An example of these incentives is contracting the services of DERs as alternatives to gird capacity enhancement to manage congestions in the distribution grid where companies can retain a percentage of their costs savings during the regulatory period.

[4] The situation is different in developing countries. In most developing countries, distribution utilities are bundled and have severe financial issues to high level of technical and commercial energy losses, mismanagement and non-cost-reflective tariffs. Distribution system operators thus often resist the growth of DERs because of the risk of further financial underperformance for them as consumers start to adopt distributed energy technologies.

is uncertainty about whether forced ownership unbundling can improve network service quality or retail competition, but the associated one-off and structural costs of unbundling are certain.

The authors suggest that instead of forced ownership unbundling, the regulator should focus on a range of measures to improve network service quality and retail competition. These include, for example, improving the quality of regulation and network performance evaluation, lowering barriers to entry for new retail suppliers, better ring fencing of distribution sector activities, improving transparency, and easing access to tariff and cost information for consumers.

Overall, to the extent that better regulation and incentives can promote retail competition and service quality at the distribution sector, ownership unbundling might not be necessary. This is especially true considering the cost of ownership unbundling and the fact that network assets constitute the lion's share by value of the balance sheet of distribution utilities. This is likely to give rise to resistance by these companies against forced ownership unbundling.

8.4 Information and Data Management in the Era of Decentralisation and Digitalisation

As smart meters and digital technologies penetrate in the distribution sector, the amount of data available increases significantly. This data is both of technical and commercial value. The commercial aspect implies restriction in access to commercially relevant data affects the competition. Asymmetric information regarding the technical condition of the network leads to barriers to entry and friction in the market. Any new supplier who wishes to enter the market needs to have access to some degrees of customer information such as their consumption, tariff, etc., to estimate the cost of its supply and design its business strategy. A distributed generation efficient siting and generation require access to information about network condition and other commercially relevant data. In a similar way, aggregation business is contingent upon access to data about distributed energy resources.[5] Indeed, most emerging business models at the distribution sector are data driven.

---

[5] By bundling and controlling resources such as rooftop solar PV, residential home batteries, cooling/heating devices, demand response, electric vehicles charging stations, etc., in real time, the aggregator can create a so-called virtual power plant (VPP) which is

Therefore, the governance of information and data management is an important part of the restructuring initiatives and unbundling at the electricity distribution sector level. Indeed, Pérez-Arriaga et al. (2016) suggests that along with the network operation, system operation and market platform, data is the fourth dimension of electricity sector for which we need to define the responsibility of handling and conditions for access. The authors suggest establishing a data hub with the responsibility of secure storage of metered consumers' data, data on network operation and constraints and other commercially relevant data. The hub then is required to provide non-discriminatory access to these data to end users and other market participants while ensuring privacy of individual consumers' and other market agents' information.

Given the presence of economies of scope between metering, system operation, and data access, one argument is to combine the responsibility of data hub manager with the distribution system operation if the condition of an independent DSO can be met (Pe'rez-Arriaga et al., 2016). An independent DSO has no interest in commercial activities and thus little incentive to discriminate against access to relevant data. In the absence of independence of distribution system operation from competitive activities, the responsibility of information and data management can be delegated to an independent entity.

As data governance structure has implications for coordination and competition in the electricity supply chain, a set of principles against which a specific institutional framework of information and data management can be evaluated is needed. Brandstätt et al. (2016) define these criteria as equal access, non-discrimination, maximising coordination, and minimising regulatory and administrative efforts.

Equal access and non-discrimination are critical aspects of competition. The essence of the challenge in this context is how to balance between competition and coordination. In a regulated model of governance where the responsibility of information and data management is delegated to DSO or an energy service utility, a high level of coordination can be achieved especially if there are some degrees of vertical integration. The downside is that such an arrangement has the potential for discrimination against competitors. A market-based approach—e.g.,

---

capable of providing services to the wholesale market, retail market, or electricity network operators (both transmission and distribution).

having an independent entity in charge of data management—can potentially solve the challenge of discrimination for access to data. However, to the extent that such an approach requires ownership unbundling of the incumbent or the presence of efficient pricing across the whole distribution system, inadequate coordination will remain the biggest weakness of this governing structure.

To reconcile neutrality with efficiency, Brandstätt et al. (2016) suggest establishing a Common Information Platform (CIP). As opposed to the unbundling of network ownership, CIP unbundles information and data management with a common governance structure inclusive of all stakeholders. This approach might work better as it theoretically aligns the incentives of all parties. However, creating a consensus across stakeholders to establish such an entity, regulating CIP and designing protocols of communications and data exchange with the system operator might not be easy tasks.

Overall, it is important to address the issue of data governance in a most efficient way otherwise the increased complexity of distribution grid architecture may raise friction and hamper competition in local markets. With the rapid proliferation of DERs, distribution grid is starting to have numerous points of power injection as well as millions of points of consumption. Devices located on consumers' premises have become part of the so-called 'extended grid'. These all mean that we need to rethink regulation and the governance of market operation, system operation, and data management in this segment of the electricity supply chain.

8.5 Conclusions

The restructuring of electricity supply industry during the liberalisation era has resulted in separation of potentially competitive businesses (i.e., generation and retail) from natural monopolies (i.e., networks). The primary reasons for unbundling of the sector has been to increase competition, prevent cross subsidisation between regulated and non-regulated activities and to make network companies focus only on their network business and in this way improve efficiency and quality of their service. This logic has been applied to both electricity transmission and distribution networks even though the two networks differ significantly.

Although unbundling at the distribution level might reduce any potential cost saving from economies of scope (between distribution and retailing), the policy assumption is that the gain from increased retail competition and economies of scale through merging distribution companies can outweigh any potential loss from reducing the scope of operation of distribution networks. If unbundling of distribution networks in practice leads to increased competition, removal of cross subsidisation, and increased efficiency of DSOs, this is beneficial for consumers and industry as a whole. However, there is uncertainty whether unbundling provides benefits under all circumstances. For example, in relation to smaller network firms, the loss of economy of scope is likely to be higher than any potential gain that might be achieved through unbundling. Furthermore, as opposed to the transmission system, the benefits of separation of system operation from network ownership at the distribution level is also not clear.

There is also little evidence that ownership unbundling at the distribution level is beneficial to the power system (it might be even harmful when it is forced upon network companies). This is because it not only involves costs and formal change in the property rights and governance of distribution networks but also it might lead to an inefficient level of vertical integration (between generation and retail supply) with consequences for competition and hedging in the retail market.

Restructuring at the distribution level needs to be robust to future technological change in this segment of electricity supply chain. Specifically, with the growth of distributed energy resources and digital technologies, data has become an important part of the distribution network operation. A fair access to technically and commercially relevant data is crucial for competition and emergence of new business models at the distribution level. The unbundling of distribution networks does not need to be similar to that of the transmission system although useful lessons can be drawn from experiences at the bulk power system. Overall, an effective regulatory framework might be a substitute for hard unbundling at the distribution level. We investigate the issue of network regulation in the next chapter.

References

Baarsma, B., de Nooij, M., Koster, W., & van der Weijden, C. (2007). Divide and rule. The economic and legal implications of the proposed ownership unbundling of distribution and supply companies in the Dutch electricity sector. *Energy Policy, 35*(3), 1785–1794.

Brandstätt, C., Brunekreeft, G., Buchmann, M., & Friedrichsen, N. (2016). Balancing between competition and coordination in smart grids—A Common Information Platform (CIP). *Economics of Energy & Environmental Policy*, 6(1), 93–109.

Brunekreeft, G. (2015). Network unbundling and flawed coordination: Experience from the electricity sector. *Utilities Policy, 34*, 11–18.

Brunekreeft, G., & Ehlers, E. (2006). Ownership unbundling of electricity distribution networks and distributed generation. *Competition and Regulation in Network Industries, 1*(1), 63–86. https://doi.org/10.1177/178359170600100104

Burger, S., Jenkins, J., Batlle, C., & Pérez-Arriaga, I. (2019). Restructuring revisited part 1: Competition in electricity distribution systems. *The Energy Journal, 40*(3), 31–54.

Jamasb, T., Nepal, R., & Timilsina, G. (2017). A quarter century effort yet to come of age: A survey of electricity sector reform in developing countries. *The Energy Journal, 38*(3), 195–234.

Nillesen, P., & Pollitt, M. (2019). *Ownership unbundling of electricity distribution networks* (EPRG Working Paper 1905).

Pérez-Arriaga, I. J., Knittel, C., Miller, R., et al. (2016). *Utility of the future: An MIT energy initiative response to an industry in transition*. MIT Energy Initiative, Massachusetts Institute of Technology. Available at: http://energy.mit.edu/uof

Poudineh, R., & Jamasb, T. (2014). Distributed generation, storage, demand response and energy efficiency as alternatives to grid capacity enhancement. *Energy Policy, 67*, 222–231.

CHAPTER 9

Economic Regulation of Electricity Distribution Networks

Abstract Traditionally, the regulation of electricity networks was concerned mainly with revenue sufficiency, cost efficiency, and service quality. However, the transition of the electricity system means that economic regulation needs to align the operation of networks with wider decarbonisation objectives. Economic incentives provided to network firms need to create value for the society by encouraging them to engage in activities that facilitate the whole system optimisation and maximise the value of the network. Strong emphasis on short-run cost efficiency can result in reduction of technological and business model innovation at the network segment. Innovation is not only costly but also risky. This means regulatory frameworks need to consider the level of risk to which network companies are exposed to for their stage of innovation activity.

Keywords Economic regulation · Electricity distribution networks · Incentive regulation · Rate-of-return regulation · RIIO model

9.1 Introduction

During most of the last century the structure of the electricity supply industry was based on a vertically integrated monopoly, which owned and operated the entire supply chain from generation and transmission to distribution and retail supply. This structure was predominantly underpinned by economies of scale and installation of large-scale centralised technologies. This is because as the number of consumers supplied by a utility increases, reserve margin requirements decrease—i.e., the grouping of heterogeneous consumers effectively pools the risk—consequently, unit costs decline as output increases (Steiner, 2000).

Competition policies do not allow for the emergence of monopolies and in places that they exist, for historical or technical reasons, they are subject to regulation. Unregulated monopolies charge prices that exceed marginal costs, leading to supernormal profits, and a deadweight loss—a portion of which represents a loss in consumer welfare (consumer surplus). In competitive markets, supernormal profits tend to attract new firms, but the integrated structure of the electricity industry for most of the twentieth century presented a barrier to entry—leaving no scope for competition. Furthermore, monopolistic pricing and structure of operations resulted in both allocative[1] and productive inefficiency[2]—the latter because a monopoly has no incentive to produce at the lowest point on the average cost curve. Furthermore, as public ownership is diffuse, it is difficult to align the objectives of owners (the state) with managers; state-owned monopolies are also unable to apply hard budget constraints (Schmidt, 1996; Shleifer, 1998; Triebs & Pollitt, 2017). These inefficiencies had a direct impact on investment in the electricity sector. A state-owned monopoly which is subject to a national budget constraint or to other external pressures, may not invest sufficiently to meet its social objectives.

The problem of insufficient investment along with the technological improvement which resulted in reduction in the optimum size of generation assets from thousands of MW to few hundred MW led to revisiting the monopoly status of electricity supply industry. Therefore, many

---

[1] Price (P) was set higher than marginal cost (MC), as opposed to a perfectly competitive market in which P = MC.

[2] The firm's profit maximising output is less than the output associated with minimum average cost.

governments embarked on plans to reform the electricity supply industry by opening the sector to independent (private) generators and retailers, with the underpinning objective of improving productive efficiency in the overall electricity sector. This effectively resulted in separation of the network segment (transmission and distribution) from generation and retail supply.

However, competition is not feasible across all elements of the electricity supply chain. The technological characteristics of the electricity networks mean that they remain under natural monopoly status. A natural monopoly is an economic entity that exhibits large economies of scale given the size of the market. This implies that the duplication of network infrastructure is uneconomical. The presence of natural monopoly thus necessitates the introduction of an independent regulation over the network companies, based on a set of criteria such as cost efficiency, service reliability, etc.

This chapter reviews the evolution of economic regulation of electricity distribution networks and highlights the key issues and options with respect to incentive for innovation in network companies. The next section surveys traditional regulatory models of network utilities. Section 9.3 discusses how the rise of digitalisation, decarbonisation, and decentralisation has led to inadequacy of traditional regulatory models of electricity distribution networks. Section 9.4 discusses new thinking in the economic regulation of electricity networks. Finally, Sect. 9.5 provides the concluding remarks.

9.2 Traditional Regulatory Models of Electricity Distribution Networks

Economic regulation aims to provide incentive for the natural monopoly network utilities to behave as if they are in a competitive market. However, in practice, incentivising cost efficiency and service quality improvement in network utilities, considering the presence of information asymmetry between the regulator and the network company, is not a trivial task.

In its simplest form, information asymmetry has two important implications (Joskow, 2014). First, the firm true cost opportunities are unknown to regulator although he might have some information about their probability distribution. The cost opportunities of network utility can be high or low depending on the production technology used, exogenous cost drivers which vary across time and space, etc. Regulator's imperfect information can often be summarised as a probability distribution over a range of cost opportunities within which the regulated utility's actual cost lies. This basically means a social welfare maximising regulator faces a problem to distinguish between firms with high-cost opportunities and those with low-cost opportunities (this problem is known as 'adverse selection' in the economic literature).

The second problem is that the level and extent of managerial efforts of a regulated utility to reduce costs and improve quality of its service is unobservable to the regulator. This is important because in most circumstances there is a correlation between the amount of managerial effort and the actual cost of network firms. Thus, the regulator faces a problem known as 'moral hazard' which is related to variation of managerial effort in response to incentive provided by regulators.

The uncertainties associated with firm's cost opportunities and its managerial efforts give the firm a strategic informational advantage[3] (Joskow, 2014). The firm would like to convince the regulator that it has high-cost opportunities, so the regulator sets a high price on its regulated activities. The regulator, on the other hand, looks for a regulatory model that takes the social cost of adverse selection and moral hazard into account subject to the network utility's budget balanced constraint.

The traditional regulatory models of network companies to address the issues of adverse selection and moral hazard can be explained by two polar approaches (Joskow, 2014). On one side of the spectrum is the cost-of-service regulation (or rate-of-return regulation) which sets the price equal to the network utility's ex-post realised costs.[4] This potentially solves the issue of adverse selection as firms are compensated based on their actual cost of production and there is no extra profit. However, the main disadvantage of this model is that it does not induce managerial effort for cost efficiency thus the problem of moral hazard remains unaddressed. Although there is no excess profit in this model, consumers end up paying more here compared with a regulatory model in which some level of rent

---

[3] The regulator can take measures such as auditing and benchmarking to reduce its information disadvantage to some extent, but it will not go away completely.

[4] We assume that the commitment by regulator is credible and there is no ex-post negotiation.

is left with the network firm in order to encourage higher managerial effort.

On the other side of the spectrum is a price cap (or revenue cap) model which sets a price that can technically remain fixed forever. However, in practice, it is often started with a fixed price which is then adjusted for uncontrollable factors (e.g., the increase in input prices of the firm) and performance benchmark (e.g., the ability of the firm to improve its efficiency compared to an average firm in the industry). The main aim of this scheme is to provide incentive for managerial effort by giving an equitable share of the gain to high performance firms and consequently provide the product with lower prices to the consumers. An advantage of the price-cap regulation is that it decreases administrative costs of the rate-of-return regulation.

The price-cap policy has been implemented in several regulated industries of the UK for many years. This includes electricity sector before new regulatory model, RIIO, for network utilities was introduced in 2013. Analysing the profits and returns to investors in BT, British Gas and the water and sewerage companies, Parker (1997) concludes that this regulatory model has been generally effective in promoting cost saving but efficiency gain varies across industries.[5] An important point to consider here is that although price-cap may generally promote investments for cost reduction but if the cap declines rapidly, it may not result in such investment (Cabral & Riordan, 1989). Furthermore, cost reduction may come at the cost of deterioration of service quality if too much emphasis is placed on cost efficiency gain.

Therefore, it is important to design the price-cap regulation such that there are explicit incentives for service quality. Although there is often a positive relationship between electricity network reliability and the extent to which the firm is allowed to pass such costs to consumers (Fraser, 1994), the widely used approach is a reward-penalty mechanism that incentivises the network firm to prevent service quality falling below the minimum level required.

The question of which regulatory framework better ensures service quality depends on many factors. This is because the relationship between efficiency, reliability, and the type of regulation is not straightforward.

---

[5] According to the author 'while there is evidence that returns have fallen to a normal level at BT, they appear to have declined well below a normal level in British Gas' (page 312).

Overall, if service quality improvement requires new investment, price-cap regulation might reduce both costs and service quality (Kidokoro, 2002). However, if improving service quality requires more managerial effort, the price-cap regulation can lower costs but improve the service quality. Therefore, there is a view that given the service quality regulation is complex to design, implement, and administer, and incurs a significant cost which sometime is higher than the benefit of price-cap regulation, cost-of-service regulation might be a better choice as far as quality of the service is concerned (see Ajodhia & Hakvoort, 2005). There is another view, however, that a hybrid of price-cap and cost-of-service regulations might be more effective in this context (see Kidokoro, 2002).

Information asymmetry is at the heart of challenges that regulator faces when regulating firm's cost and service quality. One way for regulator to reduce its informational disadvantage is to adopt a yardstick competition scheme as suggested by Shleifer (1985). Such a scheme also provides a way to combine price-cap and rate-of-return regulation. Indeed, the allowed revenue of the network firm can be a combination of its actual cost and a benchmark cost. The benchmark cost can be the average or efficient cost of firms that are active in the sector. In this way, yardstick competition induces some sort of artificial competition among regulated firms.

Benchmarking can also be used to introduce a reward-penalty scheme for outputs such as the service quality. For example, the regulator can compare the performance of regulated firms with that of the reference firm and then reward or penalise them based on their outperformance or underperformance of the reference target (Jamasb & Pollitt, 2001).

Despite the appealing characteristics of benchmarking, this approach has its own issues and considerations. Identifying the reference firm through statistical methods is sensitive to shocks and errors in data, especially when cross-sectional data is used. Furthermore, if the reference firm is the most cost-efficient firm in the sector, it does not necessarily result in a benchmarking process that guarantees a high level of the service quality. This is mainly because of the issue mentioned earlier that the incentive for cost reduction might come at the cost of undermining the service quality. As a result, quality-based indicators should be integrated in cost-analysis models and this integration is preferable to cost-only approaches (Giannakis et al., 2005).

9.3 Digitalisation, Decentralisation, and Decarbonisation and Their Implications for Regulation of Electricity Networks

Electricity networks have been historically evolved to transfer electricity from a small number of large power plants to a large number of small consumers. This operational paradigm is well-known and the related technical and economic issues are well understood and managed. However, with the rise of decarbonisation policies, growth of decentralised resources and penetration of digitalisation, the old paradigm is changing.

Over the coming years, the change in the long-term demand level and its profile along with the rise of DERs will pose new challenges for electricity networks (DECC, 2012). It will be likely much more difficult to manage the grid using the same traditional approaches. For example, distributed generation can affect the operation of network protection systems in distribution grid which traditionally are designed based on a fit and forget approach—i.e., the settings of all protection equipment are static. On the contrary, when distribution networks are managed actively, the network operator makes decisions based on real-time information about the network operation and the nature of connected resource in order to change setting of protective relays in a dynamic manner.

Another issue is that some of the grid ancillary services which have historically been provided by central generation now need to be co-provided by DERs such as distributed generation, demand response, and storage. This not only necessitates network reinforcement but also requires distribution grids to become smarter in order to make efficient use of these resources in a complex environment. A smart grid uses a range of new technologies such as enhanced automatic voltage control, dynamic thermal rating, active network management, advanced data communication systems for grid operation and status and interactive technologies that optimise the operation of consumers' devices and appliances.[6] These technologies widen the set of options available to distribution network operator for investment and operation and enable

---

[6] Nonetheless, with the increased significance of data communication in the grid, the importance of cyber security increases as well. This means that investment in measure that enhance grid resiliency against malicious, accidental and natural threats needs to be an integral part of network companies' business plan.

them to choose the most efficient solution which might not necessarily be network capacity enhancement.[7]

Traditionally, the electricity distribution networks have used less sophisticated control technologies compared with the transmission system (MIT Energy Initiative, 2011). This was mainly driven by economics as despite the higher length of distribution lines, much smaller volume of demand was on the distribution grid compared with that of the transmission grid. Thus, logically it was more cost effective to invest in monitoring the transmission system than the distribution network. As a result, many of the technologies that already are available at the transmission level have not yet been deployed widely at the distribution network level.

The electrification of heat and transport will change the operating environment of electricity distribution networks significantly. It is expected that distribution grids to experience a surge in demand under conditions that some feeders might be already overloaded. The challenges of decarbonisation thus mean significant investment and innovation are required in electricity distribution network over the coming decades. However, transforming the distribution networks is likely to face a range of important regulatory barriers.

First, measures that provide new capabilities involve adopting untested and emerging technologies which are considered riskier compared with traditional distribution network capacity investment. The regulatory framework of distribution network companies is often designed to encourage conservative behaviour by network utilities. For example, engineering recommendations often do not consider the contribution that resources such as demand response and storage can make in reducing the need for network capacity enhancement. This in turn affects the approach regulators take towards non-network solutions. However, regulatory approaches that ignore opportunities for innovation are likely to become more expensive for consumers' bill at any given level of reliability.

The second related problem is that network investment has a long-life span and thus requires careful forward planning. However, given the decarbonisation objectives, there are some levels of uncertainty about the future structure of electricity supply industry, the level and profile of

---

[7] The smarter grid along with advanced information and communications technology (ICT) infrastructure will also enable end users to participate in the electricity market by offering resources such as demand response. Furthermore, it enables end users to optimise their own energy consumption.

electricity demand, and speed of adoption of low-carbon decentralised technologies (such as electric vehicles), etc. This makes it difficult for distribution network companies to choose the right timing for investment in technologies that enhance their capabilities to operate more efficiently in a decentralised power system.

Overcoming these barriers requires an effective regulatory model that encourages innovation and investment in areas that have not traditionally been considered part of the core activities of distribution network companies.

9.4 New Thinking in the Regulation of Electricity Distribution Networks

Traditional regulatory models of electricity network companies were cost efficiency-oriented, subject to firms achieving certain levels of reliability. However, with the rise of energy transition in the agenda of policymakers, the issue of innovation and activities that promote decarbonisation objectives have become of great importance. Thus, in addition to efficient operation and investment, the regulatory framework needs to provide incentive for network utilities to create value for the society (Brunekreeft et al., 2020) and facilitate deployment of low-carbon technologies.

The importance of decarbonisation objectives leaves no doubt that the regulatory model of network companies needs to move away from efficiency-oriented approaches to frameworks which include additional instruments for long-term objectives (Cambini et al., 2014). In essence, this means providing effective incentives for innovation while remaining agnostic with respect to the means of delivery (Poudineh et al., 2020).

Innovation is a risky undertaking, therefore, incentivising it requires a compensation scheme that specifies an efficient way of sharing risks between network utilities and their customers. However, due to presence of information asymmetry between the network firm and the regulator, designing such a scheme is not straightforward. Regulator is unaware of innovation opportunities available to the firm and unable to observe the effort of firm's managers in realising these opportunities. To address this problem, regulator may decide to condition the allowed revenue of the network company by its performance. However, the issue is that innovation outcome is uncertain, and the network firm might be penalised for a genuine effort which has led to an unsuccessful outcome. From an economic perspective, when the firm is risk averse and the outcome of the task is uncertain, regulator needs to provide insurance to the firm for its cost recovery otherwise the network firm would not engage in risky activities (Poudineh et al., 2020). The riskier the activity is, the lower the incentive of the network firm would be to perform the task in the presence of uncertainty about the cost recovery. On the other hand, providing full insurance to the network utility for cost recovery may discourage it from making sufficient effort to achieve a successful outcome. Therefore, incentivising innovation in this context entails a delicate balance between incentive and insurance provision for the network company.

The regulator requires a set of parameters to base compensation of the network utility upon them. These parameters can be either inputs (i.e., cost of innovation activities) or outputs (i.e., outcome of innovation activities) of the firm. An input-oriented model means that the focus of the regulator is on the cost of firm's activities. To reduce the informational disadvantage, these costs can be independently appraised or compared with the costs of peers in the industry using benchmarking techniques.[8] The alternative approach is to focus on outputs rather than inputs. In this way, the regulator can define a set of output categories along with the minimum performance target on each category of outputs. The firm's basic revenue then can be adjusted based on whether it outperforms or underperforms the set targets.

The advantage of an input-oriented model is that, depending on the design, it can insure the firm against the downside risks related to uncertain outcome of innovation activities whereas an output-based regulation enables the firm to benefit fully from the value created by a successful innovation (Bauknecht, 2011). Nonetheless, both these approaches have their own limitations. An input-based model can lead to inefficient capital and operational expenditure whereas an output-based model can expose the network utility to unwanted risks. On top of that, output-based regulation can run into the problem of measurability and verifiability especially when the network firm engages in activities beyond its core business such as enhancing network resilience, data platform provision, reducing environmental impacts, and introducing new services (Poudineh et al., 2020). The regulator thus needs to ensure that outputs can be clearly defined and measured when this model is used.

---

[8] Depending on the nature of these costs, it is possible to directly transfer them to consumers or include them in the regulatory asset base of the company to earn a return on them.

Whether regulator should use an input- or an output-oriented regulatory framework, in this context, depends on factors such as overall policy objectives, the level of uncertainty associated with firm's activities, risk attitude of the network utility and finally the cost of monitoring inputs versus outputs. An input-oriented regulation is likely to work better in the case of innovation activities that are at an early stage such as R&D and piloting. However, for introduction of new technologies or processes a more suitable approach is an output-based regulation. Given that most innovations at the level of electricity distribution networks are of the latter type, it is not surprising that output-based regulation has become popular in recent years.

It is also possible to adopt a competitive mechanism to provide incentive for innovation when the size of allocated fund is large. This entails however regulator addresses the issues of risk attitude heterogeneity among bidders given the uncertain outcome of competition and possibility that network utilities do not recover the cost of preparing proposal and participating in such initiatives (Poudineh et al., 2020). This is because smaller companies which do not have the resources of larger ones might see the competition process for allocation of innovation fund too risky and thus forego the opportunity altogether.

The regulatory framework of network utilities in most countries are still in their original post-liberalisation form which only focuses on cost efficiency of investment and operation. However, there are countries that have already started to reform their regulation of network companies. One example of such models is the UK regulatory regime RIIO (Revenue = Incentives + Innovation + Outputs), which was introduced to move away from the traditional paradigm of simply rewarding used and useful capital investments to an innovation and output-based regime with a system of rewards to achieve specified goals and targets (LARA, 2018). The UK regulatory approach for network companies provides useful insights for other countries that aim to promote decarbonisation targets in the power sector and across the economy.

The RIIO model uses two different ways to incentivise network utilities to undertake innovative activities. One is the incentive provided as part of the price control review and the other is specific innovation stimulus packages. The price control mechanism is a long-term ex-ante output-oriented regulatory model that compensates the network firm for successful innovations as part of the core activities of the company (Poudineh et al., 2020). Indeed, the regulatory framework sets targets and outputs and then provides the firm with both financial and reputational incentives in order to meet these targets. The rewards or penalties for outperforming or underperforming targets are set based on the marginal value to consumers but are not fixed and depends on the case for which incentives are provided. An important area for which these incentives exist is adoption of non-network solutions to defer or reduce the need for network reinforcement.

Another important feature of RIIO model is that it applies a total cost approach in order to encourage innovative behaviour rather than simply capital investment. Under this approach, companies are always entitled to a percentage of cost savings. The regulatory model treats a fixed percentage of total costs as capital expenditures and the rest as operational expenditures irrespective of the actual share of these cost categories. This discourages the network firm from choosing simple capital investment solutions and instead widens their choice to consider emerging non-asset-based techniques such as the use of demand response as an alternative to grid reinforcement.

Overall, the experience of network regulation since power sector liberalisation shows that focusing only on cost efficiency and service reliability is no longer sufficient. The power industry is at forefront of decarbonisation efforts and networks are the key part of the sector. There is a need for change in the paradigm of network regulation from efficiency-oriented models to approaches that encourage innovative behaviour, create value for consumers and take into account the risk which companies are faced with when engaging in task with uncertain outcomes.

9.5 Conclusions

Electricity distribution networks exhibit natural monopoly characteristics because of their high economy of scale relative to the size of market. This means incentive is needed to encourage efficient investment and operational behaviour in network companies. Due to monopolistic nature of these companies and presence of other externalities, the network providers hardly undertake the appropriate level of investment and innovation which are necessary to achieve decarbonisation targets in an efficient manner. This is exacerbated by the fact the traditional regulatory models of network companies (such as price cap and revenue cap) focus only on cost efficiency and service quality improvement.

Over the coming decades, electricity networks around the world are expected to undertake significant investment and innovation in order to address the challenges of decarbonisation. The level of low-carbon heating and cooling as well as transport are expected to rise significantly over the coming years much of which is expected to use electricity. Thus, electricity networks will have a central role in achieving decarbonisation targets in the electricity sector and across economy.

The growth of electricity usage along with changes in the operating environment of networks due to decentralisation and digitalisation mean that these companies need to transform to support decarbonisation. Traditionally, distribution network management has happened by means of over investment in capacity. However, in recent years, new sources of flexibility such as distributed generation, storage, and demand response provide alternative solutions to both short-term congestion management as well as long-term capacity upgrades. Therefore, new capabilities are needed to enable networks to utilise flexibility services.

The issue is that post-liberalisation approaches to network regulations are no longer fit for purpose during the energy transition era. An important area is innovation which includes activities that are both costly and risky. Without regulatory models that consider uncertainty in the outcome of innovation efforts by network companies, these firms may not adapt sufficiently to challenges of decarbonisation.

In terms of the practice of regulation, the regulator has several options to address the issue of innovation, but not all of them necessarily result in an efficient risk sharing between network utilities and their consumers. The regulator can focus on innovation costs (i.e., inputs) or innovation outcome (i.e., outputs) or both. Which one to choose depends on factors such as innovation direction, the cost of monitoring inputs versus outputs, and the risk attitude of network utilities. Another important point is that the regulator needs to distinguish between types of innovation activities by network companies and apply incentive instruments suitable for the stage of innovation and proportional to the degree of risk that network utilities are exposed to.

References

Ajodhia, V., & Hakvoort, R. (2005). Economic regulation of quality in electricity distribution networks. *Utilities Policy, 13*, 211–221.

Bauknecht, D. (2011). *Incentive regulation and network innovations.* (Working Paper, EUI RSCAS, 2011/02).

Brunekreeft, G., Kusznir, J., & Meyer, R. (2020, September). *The emergence of output-oriented network regulation.* Oxford Energy Forum issue 124. Oxford Institute for Energy Studies.

Cabral, L. M., & Riordan, M. H. (1989). Incentives for cost reduction under price cap regulation. *Journal of Regulatory Economics, 1*, 93–102.

Cambini, C., Croce, A., & Fumagalli, E. (2014). Output-based incentive regulation in electricity distribution: Evidence from Italy. *Energy Economics, 45*, 205–216.

DECC. (2012). *Electricity system: Assessment of future challenges—Annex department of energy and climate change* (now department for business, energy & industrial strategy) https://www.gov.uk/government/publications/electricity-system-assessment-of-future-challenges

Fraser, R. (1994). Price, quality and regulation: An analysis of price capping and the reliability of electricity supply. *Energy Economics, 16*, 175–183.

Giannakis, D., Jamasb, T., & Pollitt, M. (2005). Benchmarking and incentive regulation of quality of service: An application to the UK electricity distribution networks. *Energy Policy, 33*, 2256–2271.

Jamasb, T., & Pollitt, M. (2001). *Benchmarking and regulation of electricity transmission and distribution utilities: Lessons from international experience.* University of Cambridge.

Joskow, P. L. (2014). Incentive regulation in theory and practice: Electricity distribution and transmission networks. In *Economic regulation and its reform: What have we learned?* (pp. 291–344). University of Chicago Press. https://doi.org/10.1111/j.0022-1821.2005.00253.x

Kidokoro, Y. (2002). The effects of regulatory reform on quality. *Journal of the Japanese and International Economies, 16*, 135–146.

LARA. (2018). *Report on the study of performance-based regulation.* Michigan Department of Licensing and Regulatory Affairs (LARA). https://www.michigan.gov/documents/mpsc/MI_PBR_Report_Final_621112_7.pdf.

MIT Energy Initiative. (2011). *The future of the electric grid.* http://web.mit.edu/mitei/research/studies/documents/electric-grid-2011/ElectricGridFullReport.pdf. ISBN 978-0-9828008-6-7.

Parker, D. (1997). Price cap regulation, profitability and returns to investors in the UK regulated industries. *Utilities Policy, 6*, 303–315.

Poudineh, R., Peng, D., & Mirnezami, S. (2020). Innovation in regulated electricity networks: Incentivising tasks with highly uncertain outcomes. *Competition and Regulation in Network Industries, 21*(2), 166–192.

Poudineh, R., Sen, A., & Fattouh, B. (2018). Advancing renewable energy in resource-rich economies of the MENA. *Renewable Energy, 123*, 135–149.

Schmidt, K. M. (1996). The costs and benefits of privatization: An incomplete contracts approach. *Journal of Law, Economics, and Organization, 12*(1), 1–24.

Shleifer, A. (1985). A theory of yardstick competition. *The Rand Journal of Economics, 16*(3), 319–327.

Shleifer, A. (1998). State versus private ownership. *Journal of Economic Perspectives, 12*(4), 133–150.

Steiner, F. (2000). *Regulation, industry structure and performance in the electricity supply industry* (OECD Economics Department Working Papers No. 238). OECD Publishing.

Triebs, T. P., & Pollitt, M. G. (2017). *Objectives and incentives: Evidence from the Privatisation of Great Britain's power plants*. Available at SSRN: https://ssrn.com/abstract=2958078 or https://doi.org/10.2139/ssrn.2958078

CHAPTER 10

Conclusions

Abstract The rise of renewable energy resources and decentralisation paradigm have important implications for economics, regulation, and operation of electricity distribution networks. There is a need for new models of coordination and operation of DERs. Also, the way in which existing network capacity is allocated, and future capacity is funded need to adapt to an environment where there are flexible demand, variable generation, and users who are both producers and consumers of electricity. The concept of unbundling at distribution grid level needs to be revisited and, finally, new regulatory approaches are required to incentivise distribution network utilities to innovate and create value for consumers and society.

Keywords Electricity distribution network · DER coordination · Grid capacity allocation · Unbundling · Economic regulation

10.1 Conclusions and Policy Implications

Electricity distribution networks are subject to important changes that are brought about by decarbonisation, decentralisation, and digitalisation. In the past, it was relatively easy to connect demand, energy flow was unidirectional, there was very little renewable generation, consumer engagement was limited, and grid management was passive which means that electricity networks were sized in order to cope with the peak demand. During the energy transition era, distribution grids are experiencing an increased level of multi-directional energy flows, large increases in the number of renewable generator connection, much higher use of electricity for transport and heating/cooling services, and an increasingly complex task of managing supply and demand.

A renaissance has been happening in the prospects for DERs in the modern electricity grid which initially came in the form of rooftop solar PV but later extended to other technologies. The drivers of DERs take-up were a range of factors including policy incentives and support, technology cost reductions, retail tariff avoidance, and environmental concerns. Taken together these factors fuelled a boom in the deployment of distributed resources in many grids that continues to this day.

Distribution grids in places such as Australia, the UK, and California have already begun preparing for scenarios where most of the electricity across the grid could be supplied by distributed resources. This distributed future presents both opportunities and challenges and requires a paradigm shift in the approach to planning, investing in, and operating electricity grids. Key challenges in enabling largescale deployment of DERs are related to operational security, reliability and grid codes, markets and coordination (distributed resource-wholesale market interface, dispatch, and pricing), network management, and socio-economic considerations (e.g., privacy, data, and equity).

There are several emerging models of coordinating DERs. They represent a spectrum of market operation and ownership types. On one side of the spectrum is a highly centralised model where the transmission system operator is responsible for the distribution market operation including management of DERs. On the other side of the spectrum is a highly decentralised peer-to-peer market model where the distribution market operation is managed by an independent organisation and DERs dispatch is carried out automatically based on the market activity.

Access to grid is crucial for both consumers, producers, and prosumers. The network needs to have sufficient capacity to manage volatility in both load and generation. Network charges are a means both to finance network infrastructure and to coordinate network users within the grid. In distribution grids during the energy transition era, network charges are required to not only raise more revenue but also to raise it in a way that integrates new network users efficiently. The challenge of integrating new users at the distribution network level differs for generation, prosumers, and flexible and active users.

Network charges are a combination of one-off charges for connection and continuous charges for network usage. In order to incentivise efficient behaviour, these charges need to be cost reflective. Cost-reflective charges enable network users to balance the gain they obtain from accessing and utilising the network, with the cost that their operation and investments cause in the grid. However, it is not easy to determine network costs in relation to the network use. For different tariff options various components need to be determined such as deep vs shallow costs, fixed vs variable costs, and general versus user-specific costs. A typical three-part tariff includes fixed, capacity-based, and energy-based charging components. Weights among the pricing parts for network charges are often determined according to external criteria such as simplicity, predictability, and user acceptance. A similar balance also needs to be struck for different degrees of time and locational differentiation of network access as well as restrictions concerning firmness and flexibility.

In general, differentiated mechanisms tend to be more efficient in coordinating diverse network users with a high propensity for adapting their demand according to price signals. The downside however is that differentiation can result in transaction costs for network users and the network operator. The rise of smart metering devices and aggregator role can reduce transaction costs by buffering unprepared network users from undue complexity. Overall, a trend towards more temporally and locationally differentiated tariffs and markets can already be observed in some countries. Furthermore, concepts such as curtailable network access and buy-back of access in flexibility markets lay out the path for further differentiation.

Network operators or regulators can choose from a wide variety of mechanisms to assign access to existing, and particularly congested capacity, as well as to potential future network capacity. Access can be assigned implicitly—i.e., for example follow from successful trading in the energy market- or explicitly—i.e., administratively or in a market-based manner. Administrative allocation follows historically or logically motivated rules whereas in a market setting allocation happens as a result of supply and demand either through auction or negotiation. In practice, using a combination of these approaches is common.

The implicit allocation of access is based on the outcome of an energy market down- or upstream of the network. The differentiation of access rights is tied to the design of these markets. In a congestion-blind electricity market design initially assigned access is universal whereas in a zonal or nodal market the assigned access rights are locationally differentiated. However, at the distribution level, nodal or zonal market designs are still quite uncommon.

In addition to the transaction cost that accompanies differentiation, market-based allocation is potentially susceptible to market power. In theory, both network operator and network users may act strategically in a market for access rights and thereby impair the overall efficient outcome. This challenge can likely be met or reduced by careful and adequate market design and dedicated regulation.

With increasing congestion in the distribution system and the rise of new active and flexible users, local markets for decentralised flexibility service have come increasingly to attention of stakeholders and policymakers. These markets can be only of use of network operators for congestion management or be multi-sided platforms and thus also satisfy demand for flexibility services by other market participants. Correspondingly, to those varying purposes of such markets, the spectrum for product and market design for flexibility services is wide. Nonetheless, both product and market design need to suit flexibility providers as well as cover dimensions in which flexibility is demanded. Key challenges are vulnerability to participants' strategies, trade-off between standardised versus differentiated products, requirements for regulatory oversight, and the integration within existing sector organisation.

Sometimes the most efficient resources to optimise investment and operation of electricity distribution networks are outside the electricity system. To achieve decarbonisation targets efficiently, thus, a whole system approach might be needed. Traditional models of operation and planning tend to decouple energy vectors. However, in recent years, interlinkages and interactions between the vectors and the ways in which planning and operation of such vectors could benefit from recognition and incorporation of such interlinkages have come increasingly to the attention of regulators and policymakers. In the distribution sector, under the lens of a whole system approach, DERs introduce a multitude of integration considerations relevant to the planning and operation of energy distribution networks with some degrees of variations based on grids' individual characteristics. The range of available integration measures could be adapted to suit the specific characteristics and topology of the system under consideration. Yet, it is apparent, given the potential for increasing complexity flowing from multi-energy distributed systems, that local and distributed energy markets and systems should be designed with integration at front-of-mind.

An important issue that has implications for DERs penetration, retail competition, and network service quality is unbundling. The primary reason for unbundling of network companies is to increase competition, prevent cross subsidisation between regulated and non-regulated activities, and to encourage network utilities to focus only on their network business and in this way improve efficiency and quality of their service. This logic has been applied to both electricity transmission and distribution networks even though the two grids differ significantly. Unbundling at the distribution level might reduce any potential cost saving from economies of scope (between distribution and retailing), however, the policy assumption is that the gain from increased retail competition and economies of scale through merging distribution companies can outweigh any potential loss from reducing the scope of operation of distribution networks. This might be true under some conditions but not necessarily always. For example, in smaller network firms, the loss of economy of scope is likely higher than the potential gain from unbundling. Furthermore, as opposed to the transmission system, the benefits of separation of system operation from network ownership at the distribution level are not clear.

The key point is that restructuring of the distribution sector needs to be robust to future technological changes in this segment of supply chain. Currently, distribution utilities are facing issues that did not exist at the time of liberalisation. For example, with the growth of DERs and digital technologies, data has become an important part of distribution networks' operation. A fair access to technically and commercially relevant data is crucial for competition and emergence of new business models at the distribution level. Overall, the unbundling of distribution networks does not need to be similar to that of the transmission system although useful lessons can be drawn from experiences obtained with the bulk power system.

The issue of economic regulation of electricity distribution networks is equally important as unbundling. Due to the natural monopoly status of network infrastructures and the presence of other externalities, network providers hardly undertake the appropriate level of investment and innovation which are necessary to achieve decarbonisation targets in an efficient manner. This is exacerbated by the fact that traditional regulatory models of network companies (such as price cap and revenue cap) focus only on cost efficiency and service quality improvement. Therefore, post-liberalisation approaches to network regulations are no longer fit for purpose during the energy transition era.

There are various areas in which network utilities can undertake innovation activities. These include adoption of ICT and digital technologies, creating new services, introducing new business models, and adopting a whole system approach to network operation and investment. The issue however is that innovation activities are not only costly but also risky. Without regulatory models that consider uncertainty in the outcome of innovation efforts by network companies, these firms may not sufficiently engage in activities that facilitate efficient decarbonisation.

In terms of practice of regulation, the regulator has several options to address the issue of innovation, but not all of them necessarily result in an efficient risk sharing between network utilities and their consumers. The regulator can focus on innovation costs (i.e., inputs) or innovation outcome (i.e., outputs) or both. Which approach to choose depends on factors such as innovation direction, the cost of monitoring inputs versus outputs, and the risk attitude of electricity network companies. As all innovation activities are not of the same risk profile, the regulator should distinguish between types of innovation by distribution utilities and provide cost recovery insurance proportional to the degree of risk that the network utilities are exposed to.

Overall, the integration of distributed generation and new flexible users in the distribution system is an important step towards net-zero emission electricity supply. It will entail substantial adjustments in the operation and planning of electricity grids, changes regarding the mechanisms that govern access and utilisation of the grid and of flexibility resources and it will affect overall sector organisation regarding unbundling, incentive regulation, and innovation. In this book we have outlined key issues of this transformation and offered an assessment of the main challenges and how they might be addressed.

INDEX

A
Administrative unbundling, 105
Adverse selection, 120
Aggregation, 26, 31, 34, 53, 57, 59, 73, 84, 94, 108, 111
Aggregators, 6, 35, 57, 58, 73, 75, 84
Allocation mechanism, 63, 67, 85, 88
Asymmetric information, 109, 111, 119, 122, 125
Auction, 7, 68–70, 74, 75, 85, 135

B
Balancing responsible parties, 84, 88
Benchmarking, 120, 122
Benchmarking techniques, 126

C
Clean Energy Package, 102
Climate change, 17, 92
Connection charges, 48, 49, 54, 68
Cross subsidies, 113, 114, 137
curtailment, 7, 30, 69–72, 81, 86

D
Decentralisation, 4, 6, 7, 47, 53, 65, 92, 108, 111, 119, 123, 129, 133
Demonstration, 88, 109
Digitalisation, 6, 111, 119, 123, 129, 133
Distributed energy resources (DERs), 4–6, 11–13, 15–20, 26–38, 73, 92, 94–97, 102, 103, 106–111, 113, 114, 123, 134, 136, 137
Distributed storage, 4, 12, 16, 82, 92, 95, 109, 111, 123, 129
Distribution network owner (DNO), 16, 107, 108
Distribution system operator (DSO), 6, 20, 26, 28–31, 33–37, 82, 83, 96, 97, 105, 106, 110, 112, 114
District heating, 49, 73, 81

E
Economic dispatch, 19, 27, 28, 31, 35, 36

Economic regulation, 104, 109, 119, 137
Electricity markets, 12, 13, 26, 27, 31, 38, 54, 56, 68, 69, 75, 80, 86, 88, 92, 124, 136, 137
Electricity supply industry, 3, 113, 118, 119, 124
Electric vehicle (EV), 4, 5, 12, 16, 47, 48, 50, 54, 55, 57, 63, 65, 71, 80, 83, 94, 102, 111, 125
Electrolyser, 72
European Commission (EC), 70
European Union (EU), 46, 64, 65, 70, 82, 102, 110

F
Flexibility, 6, 7, 12, 16, 17, 19, 20, 36, 54–59, 71, 73, 74, 80–88, 94, 107, 129, 135, 136, 138
Frequency control, 5, 15, 16, 28, 30, 54, 83, 84, 95

G
Generation Company (GENCo), 105
Germany, 4, 66, 83
Governance, 3, 26, 38, 93, 103, 105, 108, 112–114
Green House Gas (GHG), 5, 88, 92, 93
Grid connection, 5, 13, 64

H
Heat pump, 49, 73, 81

I
Independent distribution system operator (IDSO), 106, 107
Independent system operator (ISO), 27, 28, 35, 36, 105–107

Information asymmetry, 109, 119, 122, 125
Innovation, 10, 20, 56, 97, 106, 119, 124–129, 138
Input-oriented model, 126
Intermittency, 63, 75, 80, 83, 84, 95

L
Legal unbundling, 102, 104, 110
Liberalisation, 3, 26, 27, 102, 104, 113, 127, 128, 137
Local communities, 94

M
Market design, 12, 69, 70, 75, 76, 84, 87, 88, 136
Moral hazard, 120

N
Natural gas, 92
Natural monopoly, 3, 102, 103, 119, 128, 137
Network access, 7, 13, 18, 20, 53, 59, 62, 67, 68, 70–73, 76, 135
Network infrastructure, 6, 46, 47, 58, 119, 134, 137
Network operator, 3, 5–7, 17, 18, 20, 27, 28, 30, 31, 46, 48–51, 53–59, 63–74, 76, 81–84, 86–88, 96, 103, 105, 108, 112, 113, 123, 135, 136
Network regulation, 18, 20, 114, 128, 129, 138
Network service quality, 3, 38, 103, 108, 110, 111, 119, 121, 122, 128, 137, 138
Network tariffs, 46–54, 56–59, 64, 68, 73, 74, 86, 104, 134, 135
Net-zero emissions strategy, 80, 138
Nodal pricing, 19, 31, 33, 103

O

Operation and maintenance (O&M), 49
Output-based regulation, 126, 127
Ownership unbundling, 102, 105, 110, 111, 113, 114

P

Power price, 31, 54, 56
Price cap, 121, 122, 128, 138
Price control review, 127
Product design, 82, 88
Public opposition, 59, 62, 72, 73, 76, 135
Public ownership, 118

R

Redispatch market, 7, 69, 70, 84, 86
Regulation, 6, 7, 46, 74, 75, 82, 85–88, 95, 102, 103, 107, 109–111, 113, 118–123, 125, 127, 129, 136, 138
Research and Development (R&D), 127
Retailers, 35, 73, 84, 88, 119
Revenue cap, 121, 128, 138
RIIO framework, 110, 121, 127, 128
Risk, 5, 13, 15, 17, 19, 29, 30, 33, 34, 37, 56, 69, 71, 74, 97, 102, 107, 109–111, 114, 118, 124–129, 138
Rooftop photovoltaic, 4, 5, 11–13, 20, 29, 92, 111, 134

S

Smart meter, 53, 57, 59, 73, 111, 135

Solar, 4, 5, 11, 13–15, 20, 29, 62, 95, 102, 111
Subsidy, 4
System operator, 17, 18, 20, 27, 28, 30, 31, 35, 63–65, 67, 71, 73, 84, 87, 96, 105, 107, 108, 113
System security, 11, 13, 16, 18–20, 33, 34, 36–38, 58, 96, 134
System strength, 14, 15, 28, 30, 37

T

Third Energy Package, 102
Total expenditure (Totex), 97, 110
Transmission network, 2, 5, 7, 12, 18, 19, 26, 27, 29, 30, 35, 36, 38, 102, 104, 124
Transmission system operator (TSO), 6, 20, 26–28, 33, 35, 36, 97, 105, 106, 134
Transport, 7, 16, 18, 47, 54, 58, 92, 93, 103, 124, 129, 134

U

Unbundling, 6, 7, 18–20, 27, 53, 56, 102–106, 109, 110, 112–114, 137, 138
United Kingdom (UK), 11, 16, 20, 27, 31, 83, 104, 110, 121, 127, 134
United States (US), 2, 4, 27, 46, 102, 105
Use-of-system charges, 49, 50, 97

W

Wind, 4, 13, 14, 62, 63, 72, 95

CPSIA information can be obtained
at www.ICGtesting.com
Printed in the USA
LVHW081644160422
716396LV00004B/107